DREAM HOME

THE PROPERTY BROTHERS'
ULTIMATE GUIDE TO FINDING & FIXING YOUR PERFECT HOUSE

JONATHAN & DREW SCOTT

Photography by David Tsay

HOUGHTON MIFFLIN HARCOURT
BOSTON / NEW YORK / 2016

Copyright © 2016 by SB Publications, LLC
Interior photography © 2016 by David Tsay
Campfire photograph by Chris Large
©2015, HGTV / Scripps Networks, LLC.
All rights reserved.

For information about permission to reproduce selections from this
book, write to trade.permissions@hmhco.com
or to Permissions, Houghton Mifflin Harcourt Publishing Company,
3 Park Avenue, 19th Floor, New York, New York 10016.

www.hmhco.com

Library of Congress Cataloging-in-Publication Data
Names: Scott, Jonathan, (1978-) author. | Scott, Drew, (1978-) author.
    Title: Dream home : the Property Brothers' ultimate guide to finding &
    fixing your perfect house / Jonathan Scott, Drew Scott ; photography
    by David Tsay.
Description: New York, New York : Houghton Mifflin Harcourt Publishing
    Company, [2016] | Includes index.
Identifiers: LCCN 2015037674 | ISBN 9780544715677 (paper over board)
| ISBN 9780544715905 (ebook) | ISBN 9780544873346 (special edition)
Subjects: LCSH: Dwellings—Remodeling. | Dwellings—Inspection. | House
    buying.
Classification: LCC TH4816 .S43 2016 | DDC 643/.12—dc23
LC record available at http://lccn.loc.gov/2015037674

Book design by Rita Sowins / Sowins Design

Printed in the United States of America
DOW 10 9 8 7 6 5 4 3 2 1

For nurturing our creative instincts;
    for quenching our thirst for knowledge;
    for making us the men we are today ...
        ... *For Mom and Dad.*

CONTENTS

INTRODUCTION: DOUBLE TROUBLE

LEFT: Drew gave up his tool belt for a stylish suit and a fancy pen.

OPPOSITE: If we had a dime for every wall we've taken down, we'd have a ton of dimes!

WE GREW UP ON A RANCH, and as soon as we could hold a hammer we were helping our dad build fences, decks, and barns, and do renovations to our house. Each spring we had to sand down the white board fences throughout our five-acre property and re-paint each one so the fence would continue to look new and in good repair. There were more than 500 sections of fence, and we were paid 25 cents per section, which included the front and back of every board (three planks high), and the posts on either end of the sections. As you can imagine, we busted our butts after school and on the weekends for weeks to get the job done.

Jonathan and Drew on an early reno project.

It didn't take us long to figure out how to be very efficient. Drew would work in front and hammer in any loose boards. Jonathan would go along behind, sand the boards down, and get rid of any old, chipping paint. Then Drew would come through and apply the new white paint. We had this choreography down to a fine art, taking less than five minutes total per section. Here we were at eight years old, already working out business strategy and calculating potential profits. Doing the math, it came out to about $3.75 per hour. Thinking back on it now … we may have been scammed. But back then we thought we were cashing in. That's ranch labor for you. We definitely learned the value of a dollar— and a hard day's work. The total earnings may have been peanuts, but at that age we felt like big shots.

Both of us have always been interested in aesthetics (and Jonathan has always been interested in his hair). When we were in elementary school we would make the typical mugs and birdhouses, but we'd always make them bigger and more colorful than the other kids'. Jonathan called them the Frankenstein'd versions, and our parents were very proud of our

Working on the set of *Property Brothers*.

efforts, no doubt. We would constantly take on little projects to fix up or create something at home too. Although the solutions were not up to Jonathan's standards today, our hearts were in the right place. For example, whenever Jonathan would see a chip in a piece of furniture, he'd take a crayon and color it in to mask the flaw.

Or, if we overheard our parents saying they wanted a piece of art for a specific wall, we figured: Why buy when we could custom-make it? Jonathan would find old art that had a nice frame and mat. Drew would draw a new picture to go in it, often using pencil crayons, which are obviously the tool of choice for most famed artists. And when our parents went away for the day, we'd completely rearrange the furniture in the house. Jonathan would push the sofa into a new position, and Drew would switch chairs, taking them out of one room and putting them in another and vice versa. That was probably a sign of things to come. Mom and Dad said it was sweet and endearing (although confusing), but we're sure they probably also found it annoying to find all the furniture had been moved around.

We were seven years old when Jonathan first saw a magician perform—and he was hooked. After a few years he became a member of the International Brotherhood of Magicians and started developing his own tricks, which involved creating props. So his first woodworking projects, at age ten, were his own magic props. After coming up with an idea, he'd sketch it out and then build the prop by hand with the tools our dad had shown us how to use. He started out with simple tricks, but by the time he was 15 he was building full-sized illusions. He took over the barn as a workshop and spent many long nights out there planning, sketching, and building while the horses stared blankly, wondering what he was up to. Little did they know he was making the impossible possible. Our parents would bring him a snack every few hours and check in just to make sure he hadn't made himself disappear. Over the years, he learned how to pick stronger, lighter-weight materials and how to work with them better. It was trial and error at its best ... but always a learning experience.

By the time we graduated from high school, we were quite involved in the arts—both as actors in television plays and musicals: Drew as a director, and Jonathan as an illusionist (you've probably seen him do some tricks on our HGTV shows *Property Brothers* and *Buying and Selling*). On top of all that, making short, independent films was very important to us, so we wanted to continue feeding that creative flame.

On the other hand, we definitely didn't want to be starving artists coming out of high school or going through college, so we deduced that investing in real estate was a sure way to make the big bucks. In order to learn everything we could about investing in real estate, we purchased every property book we could get our hands on. We both had the ability to see potential in a space, and we had soaked up some investing knowledge from our parents over the years. Jonathan at that point knew a decent amount about construction (he had built his first house from top to bottom with our dad by the time he was 16). We figured we'd put all this knowledge to work and try to make our mark in real estate ... the only problem was, we didn't have the down payment everybody was telling us we needed. Well, our motto has always been, "You can sleep when you're dead," and when we were up late one night, we caught an infomercial on how to make millions of dollars with no money down. It was like the TV was talking directly to us! (Yes, we actually bought the product. Don't judge.)

ABOVE: Jonathan is either reciting poetry or prepping a scene.

UPPER RIGHT: Drew proving he's the hardest-working brother, on and off the camera.

RIGHT: Just another interview. Same as always, Jonathan won't stop talking!

Our very first "investment" property wasn't even one that we purchased. It was a lease on a seven-bedroom house near the University of Calgary (where we were taking classes), which we took over from the leaseholder and managed profitably. At 18, we were in the proud possession of a shared accommodation rental unit, perfectly located for students. The owner hadn't raised the rent in over a decade, nor made any improvements. Dozens of students had come and gone over the years, and the place was pretty run-down. (That's being kind.) After we took over the property, we cleaned it up and made all the repairs and cosmetic changes that we could afford. Then we raised the rent to match the market and rented the remaining five bedrooms to other students. Not only were we personally living rent-free, but we were making a profit of about $800 a month for over a year while going to school.

Then, we found a seller who needed to unload his property quickly, and as a result he allowed us to use $250 of our saved-up money as the down payment on his $200,000 house, right across from the university. It wasn't "zero down," but it came pretty close. We used money that we had saved up from the rental property to renovate the house, and we sold it one year later for a profit of about $50,000. That's when the light bulb really went on and we thought: *There's something here.* We immediately started to look for other properties to buy, fix up, and sell.

At first we used local real estate agents to find and purchase, and eventually list and sell, the houses we renovated. But we realized that some of these agents didn't really have our best interests in mind. Instead of being partners, they were naysayers. Everyone has an opinion in real estate, and we had to become very discriminating about who we listened to. Some real estate agents would tell us we couldn't buy a house with a very low down payment, but we knew that was wrong because we had bought our first house with just $250 down, assumption of the seller's existing mortgage, and a vendor take-back mortgage for the balance of the equity. A vendor take-back mortgage is where the seller basically acts like a bank and offers to lend the balance of funds to the buyer to help facilitate the purchase of the property. A take-back mortgage is offered at a higher rate because of its convenience, as it allows buyers to purchase property that is valued beyond their traditional financing limits. That was certainly true for us. No way did we have 20 percent of $200,000 for the house at that point. But some real estate agents didn't want to work with us on take-back deals or low down payment arrangements as they didn't understand them. So instead of admitting they were in over their heads, they'd tell us the deals were impossible to do. Lesson one: If someone doesn't understand your business and doesn't care to learn, find someone new who has a similar vision and will take an active interest in what you are trying to accomplish.

Ultimately, we knew nobody would be as passionate about our business as we were, so we put Drew through a real estate program and he became licensed as a Realtor. At that point we stopped paying commissions to someone else, and instead reinvested the money we saved. Having initially taken business in college for almost a year, Jonathan decided to leave that and go to college for construction and design. This was the start of our "one-stop shop" real estate philosophy. One of our principles was that no matter what, we would never be so desperate for a quick commission that we would cut corners or compromise our integrity. We built a business that people could rely on and trust, and—surprise, surprise—people seemed to like that.

There were still many mistakes along the way, which didn't scare us. We never regretted any of them, as long as we learned from them. We figured out that it was not always worth creating the absolute nicest house on the block in some neighborhoods. We definitely over-renovated a few properties, and it was hard to get our money back from some of them. A prime example of this was a house we bought in a first-time buyer community; we learned the hard way that there's no sense putting in fancy granite countertops in a house like that. A good-quality laminate countertop will do because first-time buyers are generally thrilled they're getting a countertop at all, especially one that's in new condition. They don't typically have the excess funds to pay for stone. We spent so much money and time making that house (and a couple of others, we hate to admit) beautiful. Drew sold it for a $5,000 profit. Jonathan put a lot of work into the house and barely made his labor costs back.

We also learned that it's better to follow gut instincts and pay attention to red flags. We bought one property from an owner who told us he had built it with his own hands. Jonathan had done that with our dad and acquired all the permits, but not everyone takes rules into account. We were suspicious of this seller but bought it anyway. Mistake! Once we opened the walls, we could see the work was done incorrectly and without permits (incorrect work would not be approved by inspectors). It was a mess. We had initially thought it would cost $80,000 to renovate, but it ended up costing $180,000. We barely managed to cover our expenses, and in fact we had to accept a small loss when we sold the place. But there was just no way we would sell the place without fixing every problem. It's the right thing to do. In fact, we wouldn't be able to sleep at night if we tried to pass an issue on to an unsuspecting buyer.

When we created Scott Real Estate, it was a one-stop shop that provided renovation and design services, staging, as well as traditional real estate buying and selling. At the time, that was a different way to run a real estate company. And the business exploded. We continued to grow to the point where we were working with hundreds of clients and doing massive projects on the construction side. We hired additional real estate agents, and had several crews working the job sites. We kept ourselves informed when it came to trends and watched the market for signs of change.

In 2007, we started to see instability in the U.S. economy and feared it would affect things close to home, so we shifted our investment strategies and became a little more conservative. We wrapped up the several large commercial construction projects we had on the go and held off on picking up any more. Before we knew it, and nobody could have seen it happening that fast, the bottom fell right out of the market and nothing was selling. Many companies closed their doors and lots of investors lost their shirts because they over-leveraged and speculated that the economy would never stop going up. We, on the other hand, did not over-leverage, as we owned almost everything outright. In fact, we only took a small hit on one property, but knew we definitely would not be reinvesting in the same market at that time. So, we looked for opportunities in areas that were farther along in the recession. Las Vegas stood out as a prime location for us to expand our real estate business; in 2008 Jonathan set up shop there.

With the move and all the changes in the industry, we were very busy, but still enjoyed mixing things up a little. We have always enjoyed performing and being in front of people. At the same time, we had a passion for business and being entrepreneurs, and it's always

intrigued us to find a way to innovate in both these areas. Jonathan would perform magic when he could, mostly for charitable events, and we both were still acting on the side for fun. However, we did notice a change here too. We were getting fewer and fewer calls for acting gigs and more calls for hosting jobs.

One of the calls was for Drew to audition for a show called *Realtor Idol*. Think *American Idol* meets competitive real estate. Seriously, it was the dumbest idea we'd ever heard, and the show went nowhere. However, the production company liked Drew, and when they found out he had a twin brother who was a contractor and designer, they pitched us a show idea called *My Dream Home*. It was what we were already doing professionally, finding run-down fixer-uppers for clients and transforming them into their ultimate dream home, packed with all their must-haves.

At this point Jonathan was settled in Las Vegas, and Drew was living in Vancouver. The production company flew us to Toronto where we shot a sizzle reel—the short, fast-paced video that demonstrates the concept for a show and provides information on the setting and characters. In other words, it's just enough information to create excitement among the decision makers to give the project the green light. In 2009, a network in Canada picked up the pilot and literally within two weeks we were back in Toronto shooting again. Once that wrapped, the waiting and anticipation began … and continued for an excruciatingly long time.

Unfortunately it seemed like we were stuck at a red light for about six months, because we didn't hear anything back from the production company or the network. *Too bad*, we thought. *Something else will come along*. Then just as we were about to completely discount the possibility of the entire project, the phone rang. It was the production executive, and he wanted us back in Toronto (yet again) the next week to start shooting the full first season of *Property Brothers*. The network, W, liked the pilot so much that they ordered an entire season even before airing the original pilot. We stayed in Toronto filming the entire first season nonstop. The show quickly hit number one in the Canadian market, and with those statistics, it was pitched to an American television network that wanted to test a half-hour version. The test went well (number one show of the night in their ratings during the test run!) and as a result, HGTV purchased all the one-hour episodes of the first season of *Property Brothers*. Somehow they were able to look past our crazy hair and wild ideas and see a show that their audience could relate to.

We don't come from a well-to-do family, and we had no connections that "made it happen" for us. We just worked hard and actively listened to the professionals around us. Our mom was a paralegal and the lawyers in her office often gave us free legal advice for our transactions. Our best friend's dad had an accounting firm, and never minded giving us financial and accounting advice when we needed it. We soaked up every piece of information like sponges, and we took what we learned along with our passion and made a success of it all.

What's really gratifying about the shows is not just that they have become a success or that we're showing people how they get into their dream homes, but that we inspire millions of people and create jobs wherever we go. We generally film in a city for five to seven months and always work with local area experts so we can best represent our clients. Drew has a team of local real estate agents and researchers help find homes and candidates for the shows. Jonathan has a local army of sub trades, design assistants, and office staff that keep all the projects in order. He always uses local trades so that there is a warranty on the work after we leave, and local designers who have the inside scoop with local vendors who can get us great deals. Typically, we create about 100 jobs in each city we go to and are always sad to leave because everyone we work with becomes like family to us.

This book talks about envisioning your dream home and offers practical steps in getting there. Working in real estate as long as we have has taught us which properties are worth fixing up, how to create budgets, and the value of hiring the right professionals for the jobs. In television, you are pushed to the extreme in all areas, so we really honed our skills when it came to being on time, keeping on top of scheduling, and balancing the needs of the many different people involved in a project. For instance, as a result of our early missteps, we became very strict about budgets, contingencies, and listening to what a house is trying to tell us when we look at it. We always plan on the worst-case scenario and make it so the numbers work. That way if the project comes together faster or under budget, it's like icing on the cake. We have definitely learned how valuable everyone's time is, and we do our best not to waste anybody's.

That's why we're so excited about *Dream Home*. All of the insights we picked up over the years from school, our hands-on experience, and from our shows are extremely valuable to any person who hopes to live in their "forever house." We're eager to share all the tips and tricks we've established while working on various styles of houses and with many different kinds of homeowners (couples, families, singles). We have a good idea of what people need versus what they want, and more importantly, how to achieve the perfect design without busting budgets. We are confident enough to share our best ideas and modest enough to share our mistakes so you can learn from them.

Dream Home takes you through the process of buying and selling, renovating and designing, and, of course, adding those important finishing touches that make a house a home. We even included a how-to on making your outdoor spaces beautiful and more livable, something we don't get to do very often on our shows. (In real life, we love nature and hanging out with friends in the fresh air. There was no way we were going to leave that out of the mix.)

GET READY TO LEARN TO:

> Decide whether it's better to stay or move.

> Pinpoint the right location for your home search.

> Find the right real estate agent.

> Assess potential buys with fixer checklists so you can determine if a house needs more fixes than you can handle.

> Make an offer on a house.

> Negotiate a price.

> Finalize a buy.

> Identify your must-haves and convey them to potential contractors so you get exactly what you want.

> Put together the right team and work with them.

> Establish a financial plan, along with the give and take of meeting your requirements without blowing the budget.

> Select materials and finishing touches.

> Get your landscape in shape.

Hey, we can't hold your hand through the whole process—we wish we could!—so we hope *Dream Home* helps you achieve all your must-haves on time, on budget, and with a smile. Grab your sledgehammer, and dream big ... this is going to be worth it!

—Jonathan & Drew Scott

WELCOME
HOME

ARE YOU IN THE HOME OF YOUR DREAMS ...
OR NOT?

High real estate prices in desirable neighborhoods often force homebuyers into settling for less-than-perfect houses. Proximity to sought-after amenities is forfeited for the style of a home; a sensible floor plan is sacrificed for stunning views; interesting details take a backseat to better locations; or the poor physical condition of a property is tolerated in exchange for the right number of bedrooms. Buyers with a budget (most of us!) often assume compromise is part of the deal. Yet, there is a way to turn a third-place runner-up into a first-class winner. After buying, fixing, and selling houses for more than two decades, we've proven that nearly every house has the potential to be improved. Even the dowdiest domain can emerge from its funk and provide homeowners with all their must-haves through thoughtful renovation. Your dream home is definitely within reach.

First, though, you have to decide whether your current place has the potential to reach "dream" status or if moving on is the best way to create a dream home with all your must-haves. Bottom line: Should you move or stay put? Many homeowners find themselves in real estate paralysis as they try to answer this question. We've seen plenty of that with our clients. Jonathan had the jitters when he looked for a bigger house in Las Vegas, where we could both live and host family and friends comfortably. Detailed in all its gory, uh, glory on *Property Brothers at Home*, that house represents the same journey you'll take as you create your dream home.

Since 2008, Jonathan has called Las Vegas home, and Drew made the official move in 2010. Drew had a nice condo close to the Las Vegas strip, which he hardly used because he spent so much time on the road due to our busy shooting schedule. Jonathan had a great little house in Summerlin (a master planned community west of Las Vegas), which he used more frequently than Drew used his condo, but it wasn't the kind of place that encouraged large gatherings or indoor-outdoor entertaining. In 2011, we started thinking about selling our individual homes and finding one big family hub that worked better for our lifestyle. There was a tangible quality-of-life benefit in having a large, custom space in sunny Las Vegas, one that could serve as a homestead for us, a getaway for our parents over the winter, and a place for family and friends to gather for the holidays. Neither of our existing places could be converted into the space we needed. The decision of whether to stay or go was easy. Go. By October of that year we had bought a house … but it needed work.

Choosing the right house was a huge risk because Jonathan was flying solo since Drew was spending a lot of time either on the road or in Vancouver. Drew had faith. We agreed on our must-haves for the property, which we also assumed we'd end up renovating because we were going to look at foreclosures (Nevada and especially Las Vegas had a large inventory of run-down, foreclosed homes). We have yet to find a turnkey (move-in-ready) foreclosure.

Aside from enough space to hold everyone, the property had to be close to the airport—no more than 20 minutes away—because we would still be traveling like mad; it had to be near the Strip for easy access to restaurants and shows; and there needed to be a buffer from the tourists and crowds, a quiet place where we could spread out. We preferred a single story home on a fairly

large lot since we wanted to create a large outdoor living and entertaining area with a pool and a waterslide. Finally, we wanted something fairly new, less than 20 years old. These were qualities we did not want to compromise on. As for the style and look of the house, we were open to anything with potential or "good bones" because we knew that we could change physical features of any house we didn't like.

Jonathan looked at more than 40 houses, including a really nice one in a master planned community (meticulously maintained large scale developments with a variety of house styles, many amenities, and often guard gated). It was everything we wanted in a home and extremely tempting, but unfortunately, it was 40 minutes from the airport. We're often home for very short periods of time, sometimes just 24 hours, so if it takes 40 minutes (or more with city traffic) to get to and from McCarren Airport, we just couldn't do it.

A handful of homes, all foreclosures, had gorgeous potential architecturally. This being Nevada, they were all red dirt landscape on the outside, complemented by Vegas taupe on the inside. One in particular was listed on the high end of the budget, but we could check off all the boxes: big lot; living area on one floor but an open game room on the second; 10 minutes from the airport; and close to the Strip but not so close that we'd get any overflow of wandering tourists. It had great bones, and Jonathan could do to it exactly what we wanted to do.

Best of all, it was right next to a horse farm, which made it feel like we were in the country even though we were within city limits. Some of our friends used to say it smells like horse manure. To be honest, it reminds us of our childhood growing up on the ranch. Plus, Jonathan's favorite smoothie shop is just down the street. Now that we think about it, maybe that's what tipped the scales. Sold! Jonathan lived in the house for three years, as is, before we redesigned it. We didn't buy much furniture after the sale went through; we wanted to wait to re-do it before we made such a large investment. It was sparse, to say the least, but it gave Jonathan a chance to live in it and get a feel for the space. And maybe have some wide open space to chase the dogs around. Eventually, however, it would become the home we wanted it to be.

"REALTY" CHECK: THE PROS HAVE TO HAVE IT

Does your current house have the potential to fulfill all your must-haves, or, like us, will you look for another property? While it's true every house can be improved, not every house, even with a top-to-bottom, first-class renovation, ticks off every item on your wish list. Sometimes the renovation would cost so much you could never get a return on the investment. The pros have to outweigh the cons to stay; otherwise you're probably better off moving on.

Funky or unique features may entice you to stay.

Stay or Go?

From our experience, about 25 percent of homeowners who are unhappy with their current home's features should stay in the home they are in and fix it up. How do you know if you're in that group? All homeowners tend to raise similar objections when a space stops working: not enough storage, too few bedrooms and bathrooms, an outdated kitchen, a layout that doesn't function for current needs, and/or inadequate outdoor entertaining space. All of these problems can be solved to some extent, while other issues, such as location and plot size, are more finite.

It's hard to move a house from one location to another (it takes more than Jonathan and his demo hammer), and while many houses can be expanded, it's not always possible because of zoning restrictions or land size. Drew's negotiating skills are legendary but they're still not good enough to change a quarter-acre lot to a half acre. Here's our simple Stay or Go Checklist—if you've got more checks in one section than the other, then you know what to do …

Stay and Consider a Remodel If ...

☐ **I LOVE THIS PLACE, DESPITE ITS FLAWS!** Some flaws add character (quirky but safe staircase, 1970s paneling in the family room that actually is kind of funky and cool); others are a nuisance (too many small rooms cut off from one another, awkward kitchen layout). Many problems in a home can be more easily remedied than you think. Make a list, run it by a contractor, and price out the fixes. You may enjoy your home a lot more ... and not have to deal with a move.

☐ **MY HOUSE AND 'HOOD MAKE ME HAPPY ... MOST OF THE TIME.** We naturally become very attached to a home, our neighbors, and the area we grew up in or where we're raising a family. In that case, if the only part of living in that place that you don't like is some of the home's negative characteristics, *really* make sure that you've put in enough effort to fix them up before moving. A warm attachment to a certain area is worth a great deal—don't forget that.

☐ **MY COMMUTE IS PERFECT.** Many of our clients were in a perfect location but wanted to move because they needed more space or more modern features. It can often be more cost effective to add needed square footage to an existing home (including building up, not just out), or to update a key space like the kitchen or bath than it is to move if your commute is a breeze and the quality time you have at home is optimized because of that. The taxes, commissions, and fees involved in selling your current place and buying a new one don't come cheap. Those costs might add up to your renovation budget (see page 48 for details on the cost of selling, buying, and moving).

☐ **MY CITY OR TOWN IS GROWING AND CHANGING IN WAYS I REALLY LIKE. MY HOUSE IS PERFECTLY SITUATED TO BENEFIT FROM THIS EVOLUTION.** Some of the best investments we have ever made were in up-and-coming neighborhoods. Investors naturally flock to the most affordable neighborhoods and start tearing down homes and building new, or they do complete gut overhauls. It's a snowball effect. After the first handful of homes is redone, the market starts to pick up. More investors look to rebuild there, property values go up, and the demand continues to skyrocket. If you live in a neighborhood where this is happening, consider holding on to and fixing up your place. You may already be living in the future most desirable neighborhood in your area, which makes your house a good long-term investment. Staying is a great option.

☐ **MOVING IS NOT COST EFFECTIVE RIGHT NOW.** Drew cautions to never be desperate to sell (or buy), because it causes you to lose money. As a real estate agent, he's seen this tragedy play out too many times, and he tries hard to prevent clients from acting out of anxiety and fear. Sometimes sellers will chase the market, meaning they keep lowering the price of their home, which may make buyers feel like there's something wrong with the house, and they may try to get it even cheaper. We go into greater detail about this in The Bold Buy (page 121), but for now, remember to go by the numbers, break down all the costs involved in moving (see page 48 for estimates), and if for some reason selling puts you in a bad financial spot, don't do it. Give some thought to what was driving you away in the first place. Maybe they are things that can be fixed.

☐ **I WOULD NOT RECOVER THE COSTS ASSOCIATED WITH THE ORIGINAL PURCHASE RIGHT NOW.** Many people find themselves in this situation because they bought their property at the peak of a market, and now it's worth substantially less. Talk to an accountant or financial advisor and determine whether you're better off toughing it out or if bankruptcy or a short sale is the best solution. The answer is different for everybody. Just remember, you don't lose money until you sell the place. We have had many clients who waited out the market, and are now in a much better position, along with equity back in their pockets.

I DON'T WANT A BIGGER MORTGAGE; I'M COMFORTABLE WITH WHAT I HAVE NOW. Don't get a bigger mortgage if you don't need to. Many people buy much larger, pricier places than they really need out of vanity, often making interest-only payments. They wait years before chipping away at the principal (the base amount of the mortgage). Be smart: only buy what you will need now or in the near future. Actively pay down your mortgage as fast as you can, and you'll be in a far better financial position for an upgrade down the line. There's no sense in maxing yourself out, including all the carrying costs that come with a bigger house: property and school taxes, utility bills, and so on.

THE FLOOR PLAN WORKS, IT'S ONLY THE _____ (FILL IN THE BLANK: KITCHEN, BATHROOM, BASEMENT) THAT'S DRIVING ME CRAZY. Anything in a home can be fixed. Just ask yourself if the pleasure and function you'll get out of the renovation, plus the resale value when you go, are worth the effort. Finish a basement, retile a bathroom, or even swap out the kitchen cabinets. Fix whatever drives you nuts. Nine times out of ten these issues can be resolved without moving.

I WANT TO GET MY HANDS DIRTY! I am a DIY devotee. There are so many projects you can take on to improve your home, and there are videos online that will teach you to do just about all of them. Remember electrical, plumbing, and structure should always be done by pros. Other than those tasks, you can tackle all sorts of improvement projects: demo a non-load-bearing wall, install flooring, change out baseboard trim and moldings, paint a room, tile a backsplash, build a deck, or lay out a paver patio.

MY CHILDREN LOVE THEIR SCHOOL, AND I WOULDN'T BE ABLE TO FIND A COMPARABLE HOUSE IN THEIR SCHOOL DISTRICT. The younger members of the family should get some say in where you live. Changing schools and finding new friends can be tough, especially if your kids are old enough to have established tight-knit "best" friendships, and if they are heavily involved in sports, music, or other programs. If you find yourself in a situation where the most important thing for you right now is your kids' current school, find a way to make your current place work. Oh, and a side note, it's much easier to move younger children than it is teenagers who have developed a network of friends.

A unique facade and beautiful landscaping are real pluses for most buyers.

Find a New Place and Move If ...

☐ **I CAN MAKE A TIDY PROFIT ON MY HOUSE IF I SELL IT NOW.** A real estate professional can tell you what your home will likely go for in today's economy. You may be surprised at how much more it's worth than you thought. Depending on your current situation, it may be a smart decision to cash out your equity, pay down any liabilities, and invest in another property that suits your needs to a tee.

☐ **MY FAMILY SIZE HAS CHANGED, AND THE HOUSE IS TOO BIG/TOO SMALL FOR US NOW.** If you are bursting at the seams and have outgrown your present home, consider moving. Depending on how much space you actually need, major

additions can easily go over budget, and become mired in the development permit process. Can you live through that? Many times big structural renovations cost more than the home could be resold for. In this situation we usually try to find the owners another home with the right footprint and square footage but where the aesthetics need an update. Cosmetic updates are not nearly as expensive as gut renovations and major additions. On the the other hand, if you are empty nesters and are rattling around in a too-big house, it's time to get a smaller place, which usually comes with lower utility bills, property taxes, and maintenance costs.

☐ **I WANT TO GET MY KIDS INTO A BETTER SCHOOL DISTRICT.** When home buying, we usually recommend that clients think about school districts even before having children, and even if they don't think they want them—for the resale value alone. Homes in good school districts are worth more than those that aren't. It can be very hard to move to a new school district as kids get older because it's tougher to leave best friends, school sports teams, and an established social and school life. If you are unhappy with the school district you are currently in, it will probably remain an issue. And let's be honest, you need to give your kids every opportunity possible to succeed or they'll still be living in your basement at 40.

☐ **MY COMMUTE IS KILLING ME!** We had a client in season one of *Property Brothers* who commuted four hours every day to and from his job: two hours to work in the morning and two hours back home at night. His kids were asleep when he left in the morning and they were in bed when he got home. That's no way to live. It's healthy for your psyche to get a home that allows you to spend more time with family and less time stuck in traffic. Keep in mind this could also mean moving closer to public transit.

☐ **THIS NEIGHBORHOOD OR COMMUNITY NO LONGER SUITS MY LIFESTYLE.** Much like everything else in life, neighborhoods evolve and change, as do people. Some changes may work well for you, such as having more useful amenities and services open up near to you. Others may have outlived their usefulness for

your current lifestyle, including living near a school (and its noisy playground) that your grown children graduated from years ago. You may have once found being near a corner store a charming convenience but now see it as a hassle because of the local teens who hang out in front. (Wow, we just dated ourselves. Next we'll be shaking a fist at kids stepping on our lawn.) We've seen city development plans change and major roadways open right behind a client's house. A commercial zoning change can bring unwanted traffic to a previously quiet neighborhood. You may want to move before you're stuck in a place that you don't enjoy—whether that's because it has changed or you have. You really have to put some thought into how these changes will affect your community and the property values. Sometimes homeowners get up in arms about light rail or public transit being extended into their community. However, from our experience this has always improved property values as now the community has easier access to the downtown or city center.

☐ **EVERYTHING IS TOO NEARBY—DON'T FENCE ME IN! ... OR, I CAN'T WALK TO ANYTHING INTERESTING OR NECESSARY.** Some people want to be right in the heart of the action; others don't want to be anywhere near it. It's a matter of personal preference. We wanted to be close to the Las Vegas Strip, but not right in the touristy area. Having a smoothie shop where Jonathan could pick up his favorite fruit combo was just enough of a nearby walking amenity for us. Everything else we need is five or so minutes away by car. If your current home is too noisy from nearby commercial businesses, too busy with traffic, and just all around too congested, there's no renovation that can resolve that. The same goes for being too far from amenities that are important to you or that would make your life more fun and convenient. There's a lot to be said for the ability to walk to restaurants, parks, and shops if that's your thing. Location really is key, so don't sacrifice that.

THIS PLACE HAS A HOPELESS FLOOR PLAN, FLOW, AND FUNCTIONALITY. There are some floor plans that no matter what you try to do, and no matter how many walls you try to open up, are just not going to get any better. Jonathan finds split-levels to be the hardest to work with when changing the floor plan because it's difficult to create a large entryway or an open-plan feeling when a small stairwell separates levels.

LAWN (OR HOUSE) MAINTENANCE IS TAKING UP MY WEEKENDS. Selling your current house to simplify your life can be a great reason to move. Whether you're too busy to handle lawn work, too cheap to pay a service company, or too lazy to do it yourself without ripping out the entire yard and pouring a concrete pad, it may be easier to find a place with more, or better, house and less yard. Heck, if you're that adverse to housework of any kind and you downsize strategically, you might be able to hire a butler.

NEW JOB, NEW LIFE! A new job can be a fresh start in many ways. Maybe your new work location is too far away from your existing home. Or you're making much better money now and would like to upsize. It may be that you want to find a new job in a new town or state. Whatever the reason, a better job (and better isn't necessarily more money—it could be more worthwhile or enjoyable work) is often worth moving for. We say go for it!

I CAN'T STAND THE CLIMATE HERE. I NEED A CHANGE OF SCENERY AND TEMPERATURE. We live and breathe this one. We grew up in Vancouver (too much rain), went to University in Calgary (too much snow), and eventually settled in Las Vegas where now all we have to battle is the summer heat and the occasional Elvis impersonator. For your own sanity, take the time to think about what you're really getting out of the region you live in. Could you have a better quality of life in another area that offers better weather, a lower cost of living, and perhaps more recreational activities that you enjoy? The decision looked clear to us.

REMODELING IS JUST NOT COST EFFECTIVE IN MY CURRENT PLACE. If your existing home absolutely doesn't work, and you either do not have the budget to renovate or you discover that the cost of a renovation would far outweigh the value of the home, that's a clear indication that a move is a must. Always go by the numbers—they never lie.

TOP TEN DREAM HOME
Must-Haves

After years of renovating homes, we've determined the ten things we know homebuyers want. Keep in mind that every market is different and there can even be multiple markets within a single city. So be sure you talk to a local real estate expert. For the most part though, we have noticed that this is what buyers want. You may find this list helpful in clarifying your own wants and needs. Plus, we just like top ten lists.

1. Open living plan with clear sight lines
2. Ample kitchen counter space
3. Separate pantry
4. Kitchen island
5. Mega-storage everywhere
6. Master suite with master bath and walk-in closets
7. Deck or patio for outside entertaining
8. Energy efficient fixtures and appliances
9. Two-car (minimum!) garage
10. Low-maintenance landscaping

Most successful
homes include ample
customized storage and
open-plan living.

Must-Have, Nice-to-Have,
AND DOESN'T-MATTER

There's a give and take between *needs* and *wants* in life. When contemplating a renovation, it's important to be clear on what you can't live without, what would be nice but is definitely optional (or at least a feature that can wait until you have more money in the budget), and what really doesn't matter to you. Lists of must-haves, nice-to-haves, and doesn't-matters come in very handy throughout the entire process of buying and renovating. You'll use them to assess your current home and your next one, and they're helpful to the contractor you hire to make your desired changes.

Get out a pad and paper or your laptop, whatever's handy, and make three columns on the page: Column one: What are the features you can't live without? Column two: What elements would be nice to have that you want to try to fit into your budget? Column three: What things don't really matter to you? These three simple lists are essential in putting your dream house in perspective. We were in one situation where we knew the client did not want to live near the railroad tracks that ran through town, but they fell in love with the features of a house with a backyard that backed up to those tracks. It seemed like a pretty obvious "pass" to Drew, but they were falling in love with the place, and falling hard. It helped pull them back to see that they had put "NOT NEAR TRACKS UNDER ANY CIRCUMSTANCES" on their must-have list. No matter how great the house—and it did meet a lot of their needs—they would have been miserable over time had they bought it. The lists help you reset and make unbiased decisions. It's like grocery shopping when you're hungry: bad idea. Sometimes when you're in that beautiful kitchen, you forget all about the nuclear power plant next door.

Use your existing home as a starting point. It doesn't matter if you already know whether you're staying or going. Form a list of features you really like about your house, that you can't live without, and then add what you would need to have in a different property (don't leave off the stuff that really bugs the #&@$! out of you about your current house). Make a second list of things that are nice about the house, but that you wouldn't mind doing without, and add the niceties that would be handy or useful in a new house. Then make a third list of basically good things about your house that don't really matter all that much to you.

If you're staying, you can use the assessment to pinpoint what needs changing and what doesn't; if you plan on buying another property, you can use your existing home's

ABOVE: You can never have enough storage.

UPPER RIGHT: Work surfaces are always a premium feature of kitchens.

RIGHT: Natural light is a must for most people—we can't argue with that.

best features when looking for another place. Look at your home as impartially as possible, assess what features don't work and, of those, determine which ones can be changed and which ones fall into the "it is what it is" category. Can you change it enough to make you happy? You might be staying. Investigate how much homes with those features in your target neighborhoods cost. If you're moving, does that number work for you? Will you have to make some changes in order to get your selling price? (We discuss this at length in The Big Sell, page 57.) We can't stress enough how important an impartial view is in real estate. As soon as you make an emotional decision, you make a bad decision. Always refer back to the facts and the numbers, as they do not lie.

If you plan to stay, use the list when talking to a contractor so you don't forget anything (it happens). He or she can give you an initial estimate of how much it will cost to remodel your existing home based on a walkthrough of the items on the list.

If you are certain you want to move, then your lists should go beyond the physical attributes of your house to include community-related must-haves. Perhaps you must be in a top-rated school district or you want to be closer a train station. Maybe you don't want a house with large trees standing close to the structure, which could block natural light and be a safety hazard in a storm (as in, big tree falls on house, house must be rebuilt). List as much as you want. You can revise later when a home search opens you to new ideas. Sometimes you don't know what you want until you see it.

Here's one homeowner's list, which may help you visualize and compile your own:

Must-Haves

> Lots of natural light
> Master suite with double sinks
> Kitchen pantry
> Practical, easy-to-maintain flooring—no carpeting!
> Four bedrooms
> Home office
> Fenced backyard

Nice-to-Haves

> Stone countertops
> Heated tile floors in bathroom
> Walk-in closet in master bedroom
> Deck or patio
> Top of the line appliances
> Living-level laundry area

Doesn't-Matters

> Huge lawn
> Front porch
> Master bedroom separate from other bedrooms
> Finished basement

This family had not yet made the decision to stay or go and their lists were focused on the attributes of the house only. This helped them determine if they could make the necessary must-have changes to their existing house because they liked the neighborhood they were in. In the end, however, they learned through a local contractor that they could not add an extra bedroom to their home (four bedrooms was a must), so they decided to move.

If you still can't decide whether to stay or look elsewhere, use your contractor's estimate to compare the cost of renovating your home to the cost of a new home that either needs some fixes or is "move-in ready." But when comparing costs of moving versus staying, don't forget about how renovation will affect the equity in your house. For instance, say your existing house as-is would sell for $300,000, and it would cost $75,000 to make the changes you need, but you would hypothetically be able to resell the improved house for only $350,000. That means you'd have a negative equity of $25,000 in your home … That's a bad move. But say you find a house in the right location that costs $275,000 plus an estimated $65,000 to make necessary changes, for a total of $340,000. And the potential renovated resale value would be, say, $360,000 … Well, those numbers do make sense. Even with closing and other costs (see page 48 for details), it still looks like you'd be better off selling your existing place for $300,000 and investing in the new house.

Two sinks and plenty
of counter space keep
relationships sane.

BROTHER VS. BROTHER:

How Much Does It Cost to Move Versus Remodeling?

DREW: If you want to move, I can sell your house and find you another one. If I'm not available (and honestly, with my schedule I'm probably not!), there's more than one good real estate agent in your community who can help you out. But before you stick a For Sale sign in your front yard, take a deep breath and calculate how much it costs to move. Since I'm a licensed Realtor, I'm all for moving on, but if the costs associated with moving outpace the costs of making your existing place more livable, I don't want you to make a poor financial decision. Many people don't accurately calculate the cost of moving.

While I can't offer exact figures for your specific move, as prices vary across the country, here are the expenses you need to consider when buying a house and moving that are often forgotten in the rush to get packing:

1. Finding a new house. Figure in all the costs associated with securing that new place to live, including how much you need to put on the table for a down payment and closing costs. There was a time when lenders offered mortgages to buyers who didn't want or could not afford to put down the standard 20 percent of the sales price. Some lenders were willing to offer 100 percent financing, meaning you didn't have to make a down payment at all. Those days are, for the most part, over. Cautious lenders have gone back to preferring buyers who have 20 percent to put down. If you have a great credit score, higher than 650 typically, lenders are willing to be a bit more flexible on the down payment percentage (and they will give you a better interest rate too). If you put down less than 20 percent, expect to pay mortgage insurance, which is often required by the lender in these circumstances and can be a lump sum fee calculated into your mortgage, or cost anywhere from $30 to $70 a month per $100,000 borrowed. It doesn't sound like much, but it adds up. Consider closing costs as well, which are the administrative charges from the lender and third parties; they are generally between 2 and 5 percent of the price of the house. Most of the time, you, as the buyer, pay these costs. Exceptions apply for certain kinds of loans, such as a Veterans Administration (VA) loan. In this case, the seller pays a part of closing costs. You can also negotiate with a seller to pick up some of these costs, as we discuss on page 137, but don't expect this to happen. You may see this often on television real estate shows, but reality is often a different story.

2. Getting your current house ready to sell. It's not just sweat equity that goes into readying a house for market. Even minor repairs add up if there are a lot of them. Costs depend on what you need to have done. A friend of ours had a list of

repairs that needed to be done on her house before she could put in on the market, including replacing two windows that were leaking badly. She spent about $7,500 getting her place ready to list, which included repairs, packing extraneous items, renting a storage unit to store them, and "staging" the house to make it look light and airy. Another couple we know only needed to spend about $500 on repairs and a and cleaning. Just know that you'll likely have to spend something on fixes, and in most cases it's over $5,000. Keep the receipts for repairs, because that money reduces any taxable profits (and can be tax deductible).

3. Your real estate agent's commission.
You pay when you sell your house, and this comes right off the top of your bottom line. Commissions vary substantially depending on where you live and which professional you choose. Some fees are a flat 6 percent or higher on the full sale price of the home, while other real estate agents charge less than 4 to 5 percent or a mix of 7 percent on the first $100,000 and 3 percent on the balance of the price. There are even discount brokerages that will just list it for around 1 percent, but will not provide any other services. You generally get what you pay for as far as services. Be sure to ask any professional you plan to work with what they are charging and exactly what you are getting for that fee. A good agent is worth every penny and is a professional who will hopefully get you more for your house in the end. And the more money agents think they can get for your place, the more willing they may be to reduce the commission. If you list your house for $1 million or more, an agent may be willing to bring the commission down a percentage point or two. However, if you are selling what is sometimes called a credit card house (i.e., it's so cheap you can put it on your Visa card ... figure of speech, never do that!), the agent may charge you more than 6 percent, or may want to agree on a minimum flat commission fee. For instance, if you're selling a tiny cabin in the woods or a mobile home for $21,000, the agent may require a minimum $2,500 commission for getting the sale done. Do the math—that's more than 10 percent! If you don't like the commission level for the work being done, don't use that agent. On the flip side, when agents feel that clients don't see the value in the work they are doing, they may decide not to work with those clients.

4. Costs associated with paying off your old loan when buying a new house.
This depends on how much you owe on your existing mortgage and if there are any early pay off penalties. These should be spelled out in your mortgage agreement, but check with the mortgage holder for details.

5. Administrative details. Title charges, government recording and transfer charges, prepaid expenses (such as insurance), and taxes or reserves deposited with the lender add up. Precise costs depend, once again, on the selling price of the home. In general, calculate that the cost will be about 1 to 2 percent of the purchase price of your house. Depending on how much the house is, these percentages can easily range from as little as a few hundred to thousands of dollars.

---

6. Packing. If you plan to enlist your friends to have a moving/packing party, your labor might be "free" (although time is money) or the cost of a few pizzas and a keg of beer. However, you still have to pack, and moving blankets, boxes, bubble wrap, and tape can cost almost as much as I spend on protein shakes in a week. Ka-ching! You might spend between $500 and $1,000 on materials if you're doing a DIY pack right. Just don't be that annoying friend who is still packing boxes when we arrive to help you load the truck. Have it all packed, be organized, and know where everything needs to go.

---

7. Moving. If you want to move yourself, costs for renting a moving truck will vary, but for short distance moves it can be a money saver over using a moving company, but you will spend a few hundred dollars for rental time plus fuel. Just remember, you're better off doing one trip with a big rental truck than 65 trips with a small truck or your own car. (Seriously!) Not into DIY? The best movers will come to your place and give you an assessment of what they will charge to transport your belongings. Be sure to get a quote based on exactly what they'll do. It costs more to have them pack. Depending on your situation, saving your own time for more valuable activities might be worth it. Things like valuable artwork, fragile items, and grand pianos do need special care. (Although you might be better off taking responsibility for certain smaller items if they are small enough for you to transport yourself.) A large piano sometimes has to be disassembled and moved by pros experienced with valuable instruments, and this can also add to the cost. According to the American Moving & Storage Association, a trade group, intrastate moves cost about $1,200 while interstate moves can cost closer to $5,700. These prices are based on a move of 7,100 pounds, the weight of goods from an average sized household. However, moving costs are sensitive to changes in labor and fuel prices, so always get at least three estimates as close to your projected move as possible. If you're moving a long distance, we recommend having a major yard sale to get rid of as much stuff as you can, which not only reduces the amount you have to pay (please don't move stuff you plan on tossing or never using), but the proceeds may even help cover moving costs.

JONATHAN: I'd love to fix your house or any other house you buy, but like Drew, I'm probably not going to be available to help you out, at least not for a long, long while. But there's someone out there who can help you if you're in that 25 percent of people who should fix up the place they're in instead of moving. Take a look at what's involved in remodeling and weigh it against the cost of moving to a new place; it may well be cheaper in the long run to update. There are obviously costs associated with staying and fixing (similar to the costs renovating a new place would require). On one episode of *Property Brothers*, we advised a young couple to buy the family home they had been renting from relatives and fix it up. It was in the perfect location, and Drew felt that they could get a great deal from their family on a house that was in a neighborhood fast becoming hot among young people and families. I knew I could put all their must-haves into the house even if they couldn't see it in the home's current state. The couple was surprised when we showed them what could be done with their own house, and bought the house they had been renting—keeping the historic gem in the family. They did indeed get the house for below market value, and they were able to revive it in ways that made it a great family home for them for years to come.

Here are the costs you should consider when overhauling your existing place (or renovating any place, for that matter):

1. General contractor. This person usually charges a flat fee for their organizational and project management skills, or will charge what is called "cost plus." Basically, the general contractor (GC) will tack on a predetermined percentage to the labor and materials as their fee. So, for example, if the estimated cost for the job is $10,000, the contractor will then add 10 to 30 percent (his management markup) to arrive at the final project cost, which is the price he will charge you for the job. The contractor should be upfront about the markup. The larger the job, usually the lower the markup percentage. Don't think the management fee is all profit, though—some of the money goes toward overhead and administrative costs. One piece of advice: Do not take on being your own GC if it's a major project and you've never done it before. Your change outs, delays, and unexpected costs will far outweigh what you would have paid a professional GC.

2. Design costs. Most of the time you need a designer to help you realize even something seemingly minor, like a bathroom re-do or add-on. A pro ensures that the house reflects your style and taste and that you don't get bogged down with the myriad choices of fabrics, furniture, and accessories. That said, designers charge in a variety of ways; they can charge hourly, per project, or percentage over cost. Like contractors, some work on similar markups, while others charge anywhere from 10 to 30 percent of the total cost of the job. You may have a designer simply help you pick a color palette and materials or you may have them handle all aspects of the project, from designing the kitchen, making purchases, styling the rooms, and final fluffing. The more they handle, the less stressful but more expensive it will be for you.

3. Permits. Depending on the project and what types of permits you need (development, building, mechanical, etc.), they can cost a couple hundred, and sometimes a few thousand dollars. It is money well spent, so make sure you or your contractor pulls permits for every job where they are necessary. Your municipality can shut down a work site if it does not have the proper permits, and you can also be liable if you didn't disclose to a buyer that proper permits weren't obtained if you sell the house later. Trust us when we say that if neighbors see work going on, they will call the town or city to make sure the community is aware of the work and inspectors will show up unannounced. Doing unpermitted work is simply not worth the risk. The city building and development office is not there to make your life miserable. In fact, quite the opposite. They are one of your best resources and can advise you of what to expect and how to follow best practices. At the end of the day, the inspectors just want

to ensure the job is being done right. Which should be your primary concern too.

4. Demolition. If you have professionals in to demolish walls or other structural features of the house (a rotten porch, for instance), depending on the scope of the work and the clean up, it can cost anywhere from $1,000 to $5,000—more of course if you are gutting the entire interior. If you do it yourself you can save money, but you have to be careful, as demo can be dangerous. You need to rent a dumpster (from $50 to $400 per day depending on the size), get all the appropriate safety gear (heavy duty gloves, work boots, and safety goggles could cost a couple of hundred dollars), and you may need to buy or rent equipment such as a demo hammer ($50 or more). The right tools definitely make the project much easier. Most injuries are usually something dumb like stepping on a nail. So invest in the proper safety equipment and take your time. Safety comes first, and if anything makes you unsure, bring in a pro. Remember to shut off the power, water, and gas to the area in which

you're working, and educate yourself if there are any environment hazards in your home (asbestos, lead paint, vermiculite). Be aware that there can be hidden circuits or pipes in the walls that shouldn't be there. If you are concerned about this, turn off utilities to the whole house. Never rush.

5. Materials, including fixtures and finishes.
Estimating is one of the hardest things to do in construction, even for a seasoned contractor. Trying to pin down the exact cost of the materials you need may be tricky but there are ways to ensure you'll stretch your dollar a little further. The nice thing about the variety of goods available these days is that you're likely to find what you want and need within the budget you've set. Just keep in mind that if you're doing a 6-month renovation don't wait until the last minute to purchase what you need when you're at the mercy of its current retail price. Plan ahead, as every retailer has different sales from week to week. Look online for deals, or even at auctions (but keep in mind there's generally no warranty on

auction purchases). You can save upwards of 50 percent on your material costs by being organized. You can also blend some more expensive materials with less expensive ones to save money without sacrificing the look. On many occasions I have combined a high-end kitchen faucet and stone countertops with less expensive prefab cabinets for a stunning kitchen that clients fall in love with. And the savings allow them to spend a little extra on the high-end appliances they might have their hearts set on.

6. Change orders. Decide to add a closet or expand the shower after renovation plans have already been agreed to? It's going to cost you more for that change than it would have had you planned it from the beginning. You'll pay a higher price for materials that don't benefit from the big bulk buy the contractor did at the start of the job (remember "economy of scale" from your Intro to Finance course?), and you'll pay for the time it takes to incorporate the new idea into the original plan. Change orders and add-ons always happen. Just do yourself a favor and try to avoid the urge. Plan in advance, include everything you need, and stick to the budget.

7. Trades. The electrical, plumbing, flooring, carpentry, and HVAC people all come with a cost attached. You're paying a general contractor to manage them, but they have to be paid for their work. If you are acting as general contractor and paying these people directly, get estimates. Prices vary across the country, so it's difficult to give any accurate averages of hourly trade fees, but as an example, consider that the average cost of a plumber is between $45 and $75 an hour (again, depending on where you live). Electricians can range from $35 to $85 an hour. When you hire a professional general contractor, their estimate should include the costs of all trade labor and materials. Usually it takes a week or two for a proper estimate to be put together on a major job because the sub trades all have to submit their costs to the GC.

8. Landscaping. If the renovation spills outside, you may find your grass needs to be reseeded or a garden replanted. The general rule of thumb is that proper landscaping for a house is about 10 percent of the home's value. That means if your house cost $300,000, expect to spend about $30,000 for full-scale landscaping, including hardscapes (patios, retaining walls, masonry fire pit, planting beds) and softscapes (grass, perennials). However, landscaping can be done in stages and you often don't have to shell out all that money at once. In fact, most landscapers are accustomed to working in phases over several seasons. Phase one might be seeding your lawn and putting in a few trees; phase two might be building a patio and a fire pit, and so on. If you don't want to wait an entire season for a seeded lawn to grow in, it's definitely worth spending the extra on sod. You'll have a full beautiful lawn instantly. This is also a job you can tackle yourself to save money.

IF YOU'RE IN IT FOR THE LONG HAUL,
Remodel for the Long Haul

Why save up for five years to add something important to your home, especially if it makes your life easier and more enjoyable? You could finance the project and enjoy it starting now. Always keep future resale value in mind. With some projects, like putting in a pool where pools are not expected (most of the country), you will never recoup your costs upon sale, so make sure it's a feature that you'll get use out of, and enjoyment.

Whatever you ultimately decide, the thinking you've done here is helpful moving forward—through selling, buying, and renovating. Just taking the time to consider the entire process will help you make better decisions. Be realistic with the scope of the job. It's better to plan for the worst-case scenario and be pleasantly surprised when you finish under budget and ahead of schedule, than it is to go into overdrive on costs and timeline.

NEW LISTING

FOR SOLD.

Drew Scott
...te Associate

THE BIG SELL

POSITION YOUR HOUSE FOR THE BEST PRICE

If (or when) you decide to sell your house in preparation for buying another, there are many to-dos to accomplish to get your current house ready to sell. You probably have a strong psychological attachment to your home, even if you understand it no longer suits your needs. Well, here's your first BIG tip: There is no place for emotion when it comes to real estate. You'll need to separate the feelings you have about your "home" from the process of selling it if you want to get your *house* to the level necessary to sell it at the very best price. Almost every homeowner we meet feels that his or her house is the nicest on the block, yet most of the time it's quite obvious that this isn't the case. You've got to be brutally honest about your home's pros and cons, its flaws and needed fixes. From doing low-cost renovations and updates that boost its appeal and value to enlisting the right agent, pricing your house properly takes effort and know-how. One guarantee: You can't live "as usual" when selling your house—*especially* if you have kids—because you have to keep it neat, tidy, and "staged" at all times to accommodate drop-in buyers.

In the beginning of our careers, we didn't have too much of a problem distancing ourselves from our respective properties when we put them on the market. At that time our investments were in the Calgary and Vancouver area. We didn't have a lot of furniture and décor, which actually made our lives easier. Back in those early days, Drew could fit his entire wardrobe in a suitcase— as opposed to today, when he needs a closet the size of a small warehouse for his clothes. To move, all Jonathan had to do was pack up his plaid shirts, hair products, and tool belt, and Drew just had to collect his tiny tie and shirt collection. After that, our properties were ready for the market. Later, our places in Las Vegas were basically crash pads, and as a result, they were very sparsely furnished. So there wasn't a lot of packing to do there, either. You might have to do a bit more de-cluttering and packing than we did. So you'll need more than the two hours we took to prepare our places for sale. Sorry!

"REALTY" CHECK: SALES INVESTMENT

Get ready to spend some dough on re-doing your house. Whether you hire a company to clean all your carpeting, rent a storage unit to stow your extra stuff, pay for landscape maintenance, bring in a construction crew to make some carefully considered updates, or hiring a staging company to make your house look like it came right out of a design magazine, selling your house for the most amount of money requires you to budget for expenses necessary to optimize its sale price. Take a deep breath, figure out how much you can spend on preparing the house for sale, and then allocate your money wisely. Keep in mind that the right professionals (real estate agent, contractor, designer) can help you determine a realistic budget to maximize the appeal of your home.

Pack up all the personal stuff. Don't distract buyers with family photos.

Get Packing!

You can get an additional $20,000 *or more* for a house that's neat and clean! Why would you leave money on the table when it costs next to nothing to clean and de-clutter? Moreover, removing a lot of personal items helps buyers picture *their* family in the home instead of yours. It may seem difficult at first to pack away all those memories, but remember, you can take them with you. You've decided that this home doesn't work for you anymore, and another family will be able to come in and make memories of their own. Family photos, extreme unique-to-you items (the mushroom-shaped pink and purple chair, large taxidermy, oversized canvas of Jonathan riding a unicorn), kid's art, and bulky and unnecessary furniture all distract prospective buyers and can cloud their judgment of your house. Unfair, yes, but most people can't see past stuff to the good bones of a space. This even includes de-cluttering your closets and dresser drawers. Buyers will open *every* door and drawer, so you better ensure you have unmentionables looking their best! That's why we recommend renting a storage unit for a few months to hold your prized but weird or distracting possessions while your house is on the market.

Take an impartial look at your house and create a realistic list of what needs to be repaired, replaced, or updated. Start by packing up personal items, keeping only the essentials. Store or discard worn-out furnishings—do you really need that torn couch or outdated easy chair in your new place anyway? Create storage solutions for remaining "must-keep" items such as your children's favorite toys (keep them to a minimum), clothing and accessories, and kitchen and bathroom items. Consider purchasing modern, simple, but attractive storage units with multiple shelves and doors or baskets to hide unattractive items. We often add storage units to homes we design, and certainly to homes we are trying to sell, especially those that lack storage. These units are convenient for hiding any remaining children's toys (we know the kids have to play with *something*) and everyday clutter in a pinch. Well-organized storage solutions give the impression of more space—always a bonus in the eyes of potential buyers. No big plans on Friday night? How about delving into de-cluttering your place? There's nothing more exciting for Drew than reorganizing his closet every other week. That's a win-win!

Keep It Clean

One of the hardest tasks for many homeowners, especially those with children, is to keep their place tidy and ready at all times for a last-minute showing. Making neatness a habit is an absolute must if you want to get the best price for your house. Buyers associate dirt, clutter, disorganization, and general poor maintenance with serious problems they may not be able to see. This may not be correct, but they do it anyway. So don't put any ideas in their heads, and keep your place spotless. We call it the *Ick Factor:* The more times a buyers says "ew" in your home, the more likely they'll just write off your property. You want the pride of ownership to show, so do a wipe-down walkthrough.

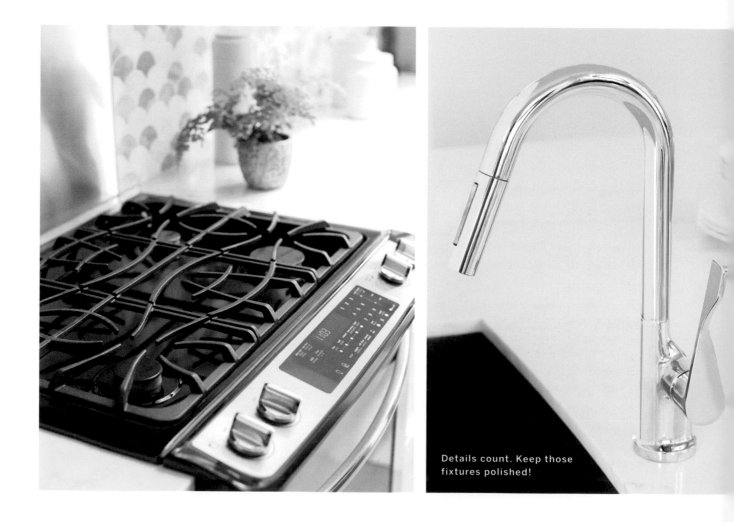

Details count. Keep those fixtures polished!

> Use a Magic Eraser to clean marks off walls and trim.

> Degrease kitchen cabinets and drawers with a cleaner made specifically for this purpose.

> Wash all windows inside and out.

> Pressure-wash decks and exterior stairs.

> Sweep, weed, and wash paved walkways, patios, and sidewalks.

> Dust everywhere ... and then dust again, eliminating dust bunnies and cobwebs. Don't forget about furniture, ceiling fan blades, air vents, and light fixtures.

> Re-caulk tubs, showers, and sinks as necessary.

> Polish faucets, fixtures, and mirrors.

> Clean out the refrigerator—yup, potential buyers are going to look and they will be turned off if they think they'll have to spend a lot of time cleaning out your stinky veggie drawer.

> Tidy up medicine cabinets and closets because too-snoopy buyers will check them out. The neater and cleaner they are, the more impressed buyers will be. Think of the message it sends if items fall out when they open up cabinet doors! Now imagine what buyers will believe about you if they see everything organized. It says you probably took good care of the rest of the house too.

> Vacuum all rugs daily.

> Keep tile, wood, vinyl, and other hard surface floors sparkling.

> Clean and sanitize dingy or moldy grout—and if it can't be cleaned, replace it.

> Roll up rugs that have worn out their welcome and leave the floor as is or replace with inexpensive modern variations.

> Hang new towels in all bathrooms.

> If you have pets, keep kitty litter scrupulously clean, cleaning it daily (and as needed) and changing it at least once a week, if not more. Buyers are turned off by pet odors—or any odors for that matter.

> Do a smell check and eliminate musty-smelling areas of your home too. If you've become accustomed to your house smells (aka: nose blind), bring a friend to your house for an honest second opinion.

> If your fireplace glass is dirty (and it probably is pretty sooty even if you've had only a couple of fires), clean the glass with soap and water.

Sparkling clean kitchens are a must when selling.

IF IT'S BROKEN,
Fix It or Swap It Out

Beyond cleaning, make sure all minor and major repairs are done before you put your house on the market. It's imperative that you keep your house in good repair during the selling process. Whatever home improvement projects you may have started need to be completed. You only get one chance at a first impression; agents and potential homebuyers both fall prey to snap judgments based on appearance. If a buyer is seriously interested in your house and makes an offer, they will hire an inspector to provide a professional assessment of any problems relating to your house. It is always best to take care of any glaring issues or problems you know about because even if a prospective buyer doesn't see them, an inspector will. Once an inspector spots even a benign issue, the buyer may be scared off—or make a lowball offer. Your house is only as strong as its weakest link. Even the smallest of issues can become a huge concern for buyers.

We know one seller who had experienced a water overflow from a humidifier that did not shut off automatically when full. The water leaked and seeped into the wood laminate while he was away for the weekend, and ended up leaving a musty smell and dark discoloration on the floor. The inspector assumed that water was seeping in from the foundation, causing warping and mold, and nothing scares a potential buyer more than ongoing mold or moisture. As a result, a really good deal fell through after the buyers insisted that the sellers dig up the foundation to check for leaks—a process that would have cost thousands of dollars. The buyers walked away after the seller refused to do something he knew was not necessary (excavation!). The homeowner then replaced the flooring and thoroughly

cleaned the space to rid it of lingering odors. The house sold in a matter of weeks after this relatively easy and inexpensive repair was made.

Take the initiative and consider paying for your own home inspection first to discover issues that you can fix prior to the buyer's inspection. An average inspection costs between $300 and $500, depending on where you live and the size and age of your property. It's money well spent if you can correct issues that may become points of contention for the buyer. For example, if termites or insect damage is found, nip it in the bud now and the buyers can be secure in knowing they won't have to deal with it. You have two options when you become aware of a latent (hidden) defect: you must either rectify the problem, or disclose in writing to a buyer that you are aware the problem exists but do not wish to fix it. Understand that the latter will often net you less for the home than fixing the problem up front.

Keep a checklist of items you need to attend to, which might look something like this:

> Touch up nicks and holes in drywall.

> Give rooms a skim coat of fresh paint.

> Check the baseboards for scuff marks you might want to repaint or go over with a Magic Eraser.

> Consider painting the firebox of your fireplace(s) with fire resistant black or charcoal gray paint for a fresh, new look.

> Replace any broken or ripped screens in windows, doors, and porches.

> Fix any cracked tiles in walls or floors (if you can do this without having to re-tile the entire kitchen or bathroom).

> Replace or repair any broken appliances.

> Check all faucets for leaks and make sure your drains and toilets are working properly.

> Ensure all doors close easily and kitchen drawers and doors don't jam and stick.

> Tighten or replace loose or non-functioning doorknobs and doorbells.

> Clean gutters and fix or replace any sections in disrepair.

> Restore decking and walkways as needed— the last thing you want is a buyer to fall through the steps on their way into your house.

> The tiniest details count. For instance, after cleaning around switch plates, make sure they are installed correctly. That means straight! Scrub around doorknobs, which tend to get dirty easily. You could be blind to this dirt as you see it—or see past it—day in and day out. While you're cleaning, check to make sure knobs aren't loose, and if they are, get your screwdriver and tighten them up.

"FOR SALE" RENOVATIONS
That Are Worth It

Once you've decided you want to put your house up for sale, you may be tempted to rebuild from the foundation up. Don't do it—you'll never get your money back. Even when we flip houses for profit, we usually don't do complete gut jobs or teardowns unless we've acquired the property for a song. That's not the way to make the most profit. We try to keep as much of the good as we can, repairing and replacing what we have to, and modernizing the home overall while focusing a little extra attention on the hot areas like the kitchen, bathroom, master bedroom, and outdoor spaces. On our show *Buying and Selling*, we are known to remove a few walls to open floor plans to create an airy feeling. We also enlarge master suites, creating a walk-in closet out of a standard double-width one or creating spa-like master bathrooms, and even replace flooring and finishes throughout entire houses if the market necessitates these updates.

Here are a few important points to keep in mind as you renovate:

DON'T MAKE UNNECESSARY CHANGES. Focus on those that pay off. When we first started flipping houses, we made some mistakes: over-renovating and adding too many luxurious features that we liked, only to find out later that buyers in those specific communities were not willing to pay extra for them. Now we're much more careful about how we spend renovation money on houses we plan to resell. All homeowners should keep the payoff potential in mind before undertaking any project. Always consider what will appeal to buyers when doing improvements. A real estate agent who knows your area can help you understand what features add value for your community and will be happy to share knowledge with you in return for a potential future client.

GET TO KNOW YOUR POTENTIAL BUYERS. Talk to a local real estate expert; look at the houses in your area that have sold, and see what sorts of features they had—and who bought them. Singles? Couples? Families? Younger or older people? If the typical buyer in your area is high-end and expects a lot of bells and whistles and your place doesn't have any, you either have to lower your expectations and your price, revise your buyer profile, or do some major renovations on the kitchen, bathrooms, and entertaining areas. If you have buyers considering your property in a mid-range priced neighborhood, check out the features that have helped seal the deal on similar houses in your area. You can get this information from a real estate agent who can do a walkthrough of your space and assess its features with a critical eye. The agent will tell you what you might consider upgrading (i.e., replacing thick pile carpeting with a lower-profile Berber or quality laminate flooring, or replacing a single sink vanity with double sinks in the master suite if there is room), and what is worth spending money on for your neighborhood and your housing market.

DO AWAY WITH THE PERSONAL. If you live in an older home and it hasn't seen a facelift in a while, or if you live in a house where you've made some questionable, um, we mean *highly personal* choices (bright green laminate on the kitchen counters or blue shag wall-to-wall carpeting in the master bedroom), it's worth investing in some smart re-dos that will raise your home's value in buyers' minds. But remember what we said earlier about cleaning up and repairing obvious fixes: If you spend your entire budget on replacing a kitchen or bathroom without cleaning up the rest of the place, you won't fool anybody. Buyers will look around and see they have to spend money beyond the purchase price. Move-in ready means that the buyer doesn't have to think about scrubbing down rooms and repainting bedroom walls, or hiring someone else to do it.

Check out the following room-by-room guide to making your house into a bestseller:

KITCHEN

GET STONED. Replace laminate countertops with a stone or composite material. Even though granite and marble are beautiful, they do require some maintenance. We like quartz, as it is zero maintenance, the most durable, and still looks amazing and natural. The fabricator of the countertop will arrange for someone to measure, template, and install the new counter, often in less than two weeks.

PAINT IT PERFECTLY. "Vintage" 1960s through 1980s golden oak cabinets usually don't need replacement if they are in good structural shape. You can paint them glossy white (or another neutral but contemporary color) and change the hardware for an inexpensive, modern update. We painted the cabinets of a dreary and dark kitchen in what was once the bachelor pad of a newly married man and his bride. The house had to appeal to families, and this relatively low-cost improvement went a long way to casting the kitchen as a place where a woman would want to spend time. It worked—the house sold for over asking price.

BE SURE TO SAND. Before you paint cabinets, clean and sand them. Then wipe them down for a clean surface, ready to take a fresh coat of paint. We recommend spraying with an oil-based acrylic to get the best finish, however some of the new latex acrylic paints come close to achieving a similar smooth, hard, "factory finish" that oil paints traditionally offer, but without the mess and cleanup headaches. If you go the latex route, just ensure that your paint is completely cured prior to using the cabinets and drawers. Use a paint sprayer for the most professional look (yup, you're going to have to remove cabinet doors and take them outside). You've seen us do this time and time again on *Buying and Selling* with the same result in the end: a much higher sale price.

LEFT: This beautiful kitchen isn't living up to its full sales potential because of the clutter.

BELOW: Clearing the clutter lets it shine—and entice buyers.

AFTER

Clean, neat, and gleaming sells kitchens.

BACK IT UP. If your kitchen doesn't have a backsplash, it should. Putting in a tile backsplash using off-the-shelf tiles (more home centers are offering bigger selections of stylish tile) is a job homeowners can do themselves too, as long as you stick with a simple pattern (like a random mosaic in neutral colors that match the other features in your kitchen, of course) or simple white subway tile.

FRESHEN FLOORING. If your current flooring looks worn, it's not always the most cost effective to try re-staining, especially if you are opening up walls or reconfiguring your layout. Matching or repairing old floors can get expensive. Consider replacing it with beautiful new, engineered hardwood. If that isn't in the budget or if you're worried that your pets and kids may wreck it again, consider a new single board laminate product or some of the newest vinyl plank flooring products as they do an amazing job of mimicking the look of engineered wood. In terms of appearance, cost, ease of installation, and durability, these products can't be beat.

FIX FIXTURES. As for sinks, replace a shallow surface-installed stainless steel sink with a very functional deeper undermount version. Replace an old fixture with a new all-in-one sprayer faucet. It's better to have something decent than something disgusting, so if you have old appliances, replace them, and make sure they match. When we say match, we don't mean the brand. The majority of buyers don't look at the brand. They simply want quality appliances, that have a unified finish. That is, all black or all stainless. Buyers love stainless steel and even perceive a kitchen with good quality standard black appliances as nicer than a kitchen with cheap-looking white appliances—and they certainly value it higher than a home with broken or worn-out appliances. We've seen homebuyers fall in love with the kitchen alone and buy the house because of that.

OPPOSITE:

1: Painting well-made but dated stained cabinets with crisp white paint and adding modern handles is a money-saving trick with a potentially huge payoff (see page 68).

2: Adding a new backsplash can give a standard kitchen an upscale look. This marble mosaic tile is widely available, affordable, and easy to install.

3: Updating flooring can be a bit more costly and time consuming than replacing a backsplash or painting, but in many instances it is worth the effort in terms of return on investment.

4: Even something as simple as replacing fixtures can make a big impact.

Buyers can easily see themselves living in this simple and sleek modern kitchen, staged to show off ample counter space, great lighting, and storage galore—features most buyers want in a kitchen, whether they cook or not.

BATHROOMS

GO WITH THE GUT. If your master bedroom has a minuscule bathroom that can't be expanded or if it's beyond dated and nonfunctional, you may have to pull out the stops to fix it. This is an instance when a full gut job could make sense. You might want to remove a small bathtub/shower combo and create a large walk-in tiled shower with double showerheads (if a tub isn't important to you and as long as there is another tub in the house on the bedroom level). If you are replacing a sink, you might as well do the countertop at the same time—choose crowd-pleasing marble, granite, or especially quartz, which requires no maintenance and mimics natural stone perfectly. You can also find countertops with integrated double sinks that are a lot more stylish than ones from the past.

GO FROM BEAST TO BEAUTY. Replace an ugly countertop and sink or vanity with something more up-to-date and stylish. Any big-box home store has numerous such items at affordable prices—sink and stone countertops are available as sets in standard sizes, as are complete vanity, countertop, and sink sets. Such a change goes a long way toward making buyers feel the bathroom is "updated" and move-in ready.

ABOVE: This bathroom is pretty standard. Adding a simple window treatment and replacing the shower curtain with a more modern and better quality version could improve it. Or, a single pane glass half wall could be added to the shower without breaking the bank.

OPPOSITE: This plain white bathroom has been staged to sell with brand new towels and rug, fresh flowers to add color, and a clutter-free vanity.

1: Replacing the countertop on a kitchen island is a great way to update the look of your kitchen.

2: Built in storage is a real bonus for buyers.

3 **THIS PAGE & NEXT PAGE:** A dressing area in a bedroom or bathroom wins over prospective homeowners.

4 **NEXT PAGE:** Rain showerheads give bathrooms a spa-like feel. Extra plumbing is required to install them, so make sure you'll get a good payoff before having the work done.

DOUBLE UP. If you have the space, hire a plumber to install a double sink to replace a single. You may not need as much counter space as you think to fit in two sinks. Depending on the size you choose, a 60-inch vanity can comfortably fit twin sinks. Once again … twins are awesome. If you're short on space, a 48-inch vanity can work—yes, even with two small but fully functional sinks. Keep in mind that the smaller the cabinet you use, the less counter space you'll have. You need a minimum of 18 to 24 inches to accommodate each sink. Since buyers prefer dual sinks, they are less likely to register smaller sink size as a negative. They might not notice the small size at all because they'll be swooning over the two sinks. Just ensure that you leave yourself with adequate counter space, as there's nothing worse than not having room for your toothbrush or soap dispenser.

GET CREATIVE WITH CABINETRY. Just like in the kitchen, bathroom cabinets that are in good shape but have a dated finish (like golden oak or knotty pine) can be refreshed via paint. This, of course, is the cheapest alternative, but may ultimately be the best if cabinets are simple and function well and offer good storage. Jonathan recommends hiring a professional to do the job if you are not 100 percent confident about your painting skills. If you do a bad job painting cabinets, it shows and looks worse than a dated wood cabinet. Brushstrokes or peeling may be visible if you didn't let it dry properly. You want buyers to feel they can just "bring their toothbrush" and use the bathroom as is, at least for a while before they decide to do their own renovation. A paint job that is done professionally doesn't look like a Band-Aid fix (something to cover up a problem in a slap-dash fashion) but a purposeful design choice.

If space allows, hire a carpenter to build a tall storage unit along any available wall space and paint it to match the rest of the cabinets in the space. If you utilize open shelving, you could paint the back panel to match the walls or even use a soft pop of color as a statement. It's the perfect place to stow carefully folded towels and your prettiest bars of soap and shampoo bottles. When storage is visible, it should be attractive. And there can never be enough storage in a buyer's mind.

Rusty, outmoded medicine cabinets must be replaced with modern alternatives or even a fabulous, large mirror. Don't sacrifice needed storage space for style—if you take out storage in the form of a medicine cabinet for a mirror, "replace" the lost storage with wall shelving or baskets. At the end of the day, we like to know there's enough room in everyone's bathrooms to store all their products. We can't stand knowing that even one person somewhere in North America might not have enough room for collectibles.

MAKE MIRRORS WORK. Placement is everything. Remember, there are people who are much shorter and much taller than you. If I step into one more bathroom where I can't see above my chest in the vanity mirror ... well, we're going to protest. To work for most people, the bottom edge of the mirror or cabinet should be 40 inches from the floor. Of course, if a room is specifically designated for kids, mirrors can be adjusted accordingly, and this doesn't include full-length mirrors, but in general use the 40-inch rule applies. In one Jack-and-Jill style bathroom (a bathroom that connects to bedrooms on either side) we placed a large mirror to cover the entire wall over the two sinks and then framed it out. That way, the mirror would serve the children in the house as they grew and could work for adults later on.

CLEAN IT UP. The major fixtures in your bathroom should look clean and usable. Dirty tubs and toilets evoke the Ick Factor more than most things. If your porcelain or enameled bathtub is chipped, worn, or badly scratched, have it re-glazed. It will look like new without the price tag of ripping everything out. A water-saving toilet can be a smart replacement, especially if your current throne is an older water-guzzling model. Potential buyers are attracted to energy- and resource-saving features, especially if it helps reduce utility bills. Besides, a lot more people these days want their home to be eco-friendly. Frameless glass shower doors give bathrooms a high-end look without breaking the bank. That's especially true if your current shower door is framed in corroded brass or plain old pitted and worn chrome. There are standard sized frameless glass doors that can save you a lot over custom glass doors.

MAKE EASY UPDATES. Replace your old showerhead with a rain showerhead. It looks (and feels) luxurious, adds a contemporary spa look to the shower area, and is an easy do-it-yourself fix. While you're at it, replace ugly or dated fixtures (clear plastic handles on faucets have to go!) with chrome, brushed nickel, or oil-rubbed bronze, depending on the design. These truly make your bathroom sparkle. Just ensure that the finishes on all your fixtures and hardware complement each other. You should never have a chrome showerhead, brushed faucet, and oil-rubbed cabinet hardware all in one space. Swap out 1970s style lighting fixtures with modern—and flattering—lighting. It's not a nightclub. When buyers go into your bathroom and turn on the lights, they want to look good!

OPPOSITE: A glass shower enclosure is appealing because it looks so clean and hygienic. This one is on roller wheels, which makes it modern and unique.

FOLLOWING PAGE: Don't be afraid to add art and plants to a bathroom. A painting or print can inject color into an unadorned space, and greenery always adds a sense of life and freshness.

BEDROOMS

HAVE A MASTER PLAN. Does your four-bedroom home lack a master bath and walk-in closet? Here's a situation where you should add one. You are better off with two decent-sized bedrooms plus a real master suite than four rooms with no real master. Take over one of the smaller rooms, and use that space for the master bath and closet. It's a big job, but money that is well spent. Don't do it if you only have a three-bedroom home—two-bedroom houses just don't have a big market in a three-plus-bedroom neighborhood.

FOCUS ON FAB FLOORING. If existing carpet in the bedrooms can't be successfully cleaned by a professional, replace it with new carpeting. While some people are OK with carpet in the bedrooms, most homeowners today prefer hardwood. So, if there is good hardwood underneath that '70s shag, consider showing it off. Remove the carpet and fix up those beautiful boards. Buyers know there is a value in well-preserved original wood flooring, and there's even more added value in a newer wide board plank. If you really want that carpet feeling under your feet in the bedrooms, a stylish area rug is the perfect solution.

BUILD A BLING-WORTHY CLOSET. Every lady (and Drew) dreams of having a walk-in closet in the master suite. Can you steal some real estate from an adjoining bedroom or hall closet to deepen a closet? If so, do it, because buyers will pay more for a walk-in closet. While you (or your contractor) are at it, give the space even more appeal and value by adding a custom closet organization system and a chandelier or other interesting hanging light fixture if the ceiling height allows.

Closet systems are a good DIY project and add real value to bedrooms.

BELOW: A simple wood treatment on the wall and an electric fireplace and surround lends a dramatic air to this very basic bedroom.

ABOVE: Restful and comfortable, the muted color palette and reflective surfaces in this room give it a serene and sophisticated look.

RIGHT: Fresh flowers inject color into a space, but they also convey that the house is truly a home.

OPPOSITE: A well-chosen upholstered bench at the end of a bed helps reinforce the idea that this bedroom has plenty of space and great function.

LIVING AREAS

ADD LIGHT. You can turn dreary and dark rooms into bright, happy places in a couple of ways. First off, add new lighting. Hire an electrician to put in a new fixture, or if the space really needs help, add recessed lighting to brighten things up. This is particularly effective in rooms below grade (like a finished basement), interior hallways, and cavernous great rooms. The other way to bring light into a room is by adding windows or French doors. Of course, you can't just stick a window anywhere. It has to be right for the space inside *and* out. However, most human beings (even Jonathan) crave sunlight and don't want to live in a cave, so if you can, find the right place in your design to put a window or French door.

BEFORE

OPPOSITE: Note the clean mantel and neatly styled coffee table.

ADD OOMPH WITH OO-LA-LA DOORS. Updating all your interior doors can add a lot of value to your home. Frosted glass doors (ensure they have a full frost so there's no transparency) can give a more modern feel and even a reclaimed wood sliding barn door can create a rustic feature out of your doorway. Just leave all the barn animals outside! If you have a beautiful yard begging buyers to spend some time in it, but it's hidden behind a small, tired slider, think about what it would cost to open things up a little and install French doors to the great outdoors (and perhaps add a patio or deck while you're out there). Even second floor master bedrooms can benefit from the addition of French doors leading out to a balcony or deck where the new owners can enjoy their morning coffee. This is a bit more extensive in terms of construction, permits, and overall work, but it's also the kind of feature that can melt a prospect's heart—and lead them to make an offer.

GO BOLD WITH BUILT-IN STORAGE. Great rooms and open plan living rooms seem to be magnets for clutter, even in the neatest, Zen-like homes. Where people congregate, so does their stuff. Cabinetry can hide wires, electronics, plus odds and ends that didn't make it out the door in your purge, while shelves can hold books and accessories with style. Don't feel the need to clutter every shelf; a few smartly placed books or décor pieces will make your open built-ins feel more like a design feature.

UNITE WITH FLOORING. Patchwork only looks good on your grandmother's quilt. Here's a rule of thumb: If you can stand anywhere in your home and see more than two types of flooring, then there's something wrong. If you see four or more types of flooring, then the situation just got critical. Unify the spaces by flowing the same flooring throughout. Go with a good quality single-board laminate for that engineered hardwood look that doesn't come with the price tag. It will be money well spent.

OPPOSITE:

1: A great lighting fixture is one of the "wow factors" that make your house memorable to buyers.

2: Replacing builder grade or standard solid doors with glass paned doors adds character and value—this one allows light to filter in between rooms without sacrificing privacy.

3: Show off built-in storage with strategic and aesthetically pleasing organization.

Open plan eating areas appeal to families.

WARM THINGS UP. Buyers—even those who live in warm climates—love the idea of a fireplace. The good news is, if it's not in your budget to run the gas lines and put in a gas fireplace, you're not completely out of luck. Electric fireplace technology has come a long way since the days of a light bulb, fan, and a flame shaped piece of silk in an obviously fake wood surround that you shove up against the wall. We've shown homeowners fireplaces side by side, asking them to choose whether they like "the gas one or the electric one," and they can't tell the difference (believe us, they have no idea). They pick the one they think is gas, and then we tell them—guess what—they're both electric. We know! It's cruel. (We don't mind pulling a fast one over on homeowners if we can teach them something important in the process.)

An easy-care gas or electric fireplace is a plus for buyers who love the glow but dislike the mess of wood burning units.

The right electric fireplace can add incredible ambiance and style with minimal, and we mean *minimal*, installation work. You don't have to build a chimney, install new gas lines, or do a bunch of fancy tile work. All you need is the unit itself and a wall for installation. If there isn't power in the right place, then you'll need an electrician to run that for you. Put one in your living room, den, or master bedroom … there is so much more flexibility since you are just working with electrical. But please help us keep our sanity and build the unit into the wall so that it looks properly finished in place the same way a gas fireplace looks. And if we see you run an exposed wire over to the closest receptacle to plug the electric fireplace in, we're sending you back to reno school!

OUTDOOR SPACES

YOU'RE WELCOME! Make sure the entryway to your home is welcoming and in good repair with a freshly painted door that adds a pop of color. Be aware that each color suggests a different message, so make sure you know what you're saying to the world! Glossy black is formal and stately, while a cool gray or deep orange is modern. Red and yellow are cheery and casual, while various shades of blue, from navy to turquoise, can read as nautical or beachy. Complete the facelift by replacing an old black mailbox with a gleaming new one in an interesting finish like copper or bronze. Buy coordinating hardware to replace shabby doorknobs and rusting or outdated lighting fixtures. Don't forget house numbers. Handsome metal or iron versions add a stately presence to your front entry. They make your house easy to find, too—unless, of course, you don't want the in-laws to find your place.

Dressing up an entryway can be as simple as placing matching planters on either side of the doorway.

LEFT: Curb appeal counts when it comes to selling. This ranch house looks like it is in disrepair but it's not.

BELOW: Switching out a plethora of plastic toys for a more attractive and useful seating arrangement and replacing dead plants with live ones shows off this well maintained ranch.

AFTER

LOSE THE DEAD WOOD. Remove dead plants and fill newly empty spaces with colorful annual flowers if the season permits, or compact evergreen trees such as dwarf Alberta spruce or boxwood. Trim overgrown shrubs and trees, particularly those that block the view from the inside or hide the front door or other features of your house. Buyers should never have to duck or weave to navigate the property. If you are preparing your house for sale during cooler seasons, add evergreen boughs to empty pots.

DON'T FORGET PLAYTIME. Show there is a place to play in your backyard—this is very important for people who have children or pets or both. A nicely maintained grassy area shows space for an impromptu ballgame or Frisbee toss. The backyard is also one area where leaving a few well-placed toys or games around can have a positive effect: think swing set, croquet game, bocce court, or horseshoe area. Even a well-kept children's playhouse decked out with a few pots of blooming annuals gives a glimpse into a pleasant lifestyle buyers can fantasize about. We've seen many people who fully pave their backyard for lower maintenance and sports use. This may work for your lifestyle but keep in mind many buyers want green space and it can be a costly fix to remove concrete and re-sod.

BE ENTERTAINING. A patio or deck area is very important. If you don't have one now it may be worth adding one. A deck or paved area large enough for a table and chairs and perhaps a grill need not be out of budget. It shows that your house also includes living space outdoors. But remember, in most communities you need a permit to build a deck; not so for a paver patio.

OPPOSITE:

1: Make sure garden beds are weed-free and colorful.

2: Toys and play areas are fine in the backyard. In fact, they go a long way toward demonstrating to families that your house is kid friendly.

3: Outdoor living is a big plus for most buyers.

4: Live it up. Creating a living room–like setting in your backyard is not only inviting, it also demonstrates that your house provides a sought-after "indoor-outdoor" lifestyle.

COOK UP A FOOD PREP PLAN. You don't have to build an outdoor kitchen to sell your house, but placing a shiny new grill (which you can take with you when you move) alongside an indoor-outdoor rolling cart gives buyers the impression your backyard is ready to host the next block party. Today, you can find fully functional grills in compact sizes. Jonathan has fit in stainless steel grills and prep areas in even the tiniest urban backyards.

GET FIRED UP. Likewise, a fire pit area need not be expensive, but it adds so much value to your yard because buyers love them. Ready-made fire pits and DIY kits are available in big box home stores. But we know of a young couple who made a beautiful fire pit with two "big rig" wheel rims (available at salvage yards for about $25 apiece) stacked on top of each other and then trimmed with wall pavers they bought on sale at a home and garden center for about $50. So, for $100 they turned out an awesome fire pit, and it took them less than an hour to complete the job once they had all the materials. They set up six Adirondack style chairs around the fire pit area and had a party that night. If staging to sell your home, the more buyers can picture themselves utilizing the space, the better.

OPPOSITE: This grill has been turned into an outdoor kitchen with the addition of two readymade prep stands.

ABOVE: A cozy fire pit is a very inexpensive way to show off the outdoor entertaining possibilities of your patio.

Open It Up

Ninety-nine percent of homeowners prefer a more open concept living space these days. Therefore if you are attempting to sell your house for top dollar, it's worth considering removing walls where structurally possible to lend a fresh, open feel. On *Property Brothers*, we often advise homeowners to change the configuration of spaces for their own lifestyle while they are in the house *and* for resale value.

That's because the vast majority of buyers out there want open concept, and if opening up your floor plan means the space will appeal to more buyers, that will equate to better offers. Opening up a wall between the kitchen and living areas, even if it means reconfiguring and perhaps replacing or painting cabinetry and replacing countertops, could be worth it if that's what your market demands. It's one more big thing a buyer won't have to do, and if they don't feel they have to do something major before they move in, they are more likely to make a better offer. This is the kind of decision you may have to discuss with both your banker (a home improvement loan might be a smart move if you do not have enough cash on hand to cover costs) and your Realtor, who can tell you whether or not it's a change worth doing.

That said, we caution against overdoing major renovations on a house you want to get to market quickly. Major reconfigurations of interior walls involve various permits, which can take precious time away from getting the house listed. On TV, we often start the permitting process before the new owners have even closed on the property, which is why Day One of work seems to start the day after the homeowners take possession of the house. Editing helps too, of course. Reality is harsh, TV is magic.

"REALTY" CHECK: 'TIS THE SEASON

Spring is the hottest time to list a house, with fall the second best time. Summer and winter are the third and fourth most popular times to list— and sell—a house. The worst time to sell is when you're desperate. At that point, we guarantee you will lose money.

Opening up walls lets your living area breathe.

BROTHER VS. BROTHER:

Set the Right Price

JONATHAN: You've done a lot of work, and now it's time to put your house on the market. There are only three reasons why a house doesn't sell.

First and foremost, there's a problem with the neighborhood or site of the house. Are you backed onto a nuclear power plant? Is your home on the corner of the busiest intersection in the city? This is rarely the case but can hurt the sale price. If you feel your neighborhood looks a little rough around the edges, keep in mind many up-and-coming neighborhoods offer big potential. In fact, you stand to see the best return on your property, and so does your potential buyer, when a neighborhood is in the process of improving. It behooves you to make your own house a noticeable part of that improvement.

The second is if there's a problem with the house. This could be something as simple as the kitchen lacking aesthetic appeal, or something serious like a major leak or structural issue. That was the case with a house we wanted to buy because it was in a great location. That is, until we discovered the foundation was completely shot, and the house was structurally unsound and, frankly, dangerous. The asking price was too high to make it worth our while to make the necessary repairs, so we walked away.

That leads us to the third and most likely problem in selling a house, and that's the price. Remember that any house, no matter how bad it looks and how structurally messed up it may be, can and will sell if the price is right. Homeowners often base the price of their home on their personal financial needs, but this wishful thinking is so wrong—and really, so random. Buyers don't care how much you owe on your credit cards or how much you need for the down payment on your next place.

DREW: It's better to be organized and know the price point you're competing against before you list your home. What really matters when pricing your house are comparable sales in your area for homes of your age, style, size, and condition. Notice I'm saying sold properties and not active listings. Sale comps are the only viable and reliable information you need when arrived at a listing value. But you can't just look at the selling price on a comp—you have to pay attention to all the features and condition issues that affected the sales price. It's like solving a math problem; you have to understand all the variables to arrive at the right answer.

If you're in an area without a lot of direct comparable properties, or if your house is unique or one-of-a-kind and true comps are hard to come by, you may want to pay for a home appraisal. Usually

the bank that the buyer is applying to for a mortgage will order an appraisal at the buyer's expense, but this happens only after an initial sale price has been agreed upon. So initiating a full appraisal before you arrive at a figure for your house can be helpful. But nine times out of ten, you should have no problem pricing the home based on the comps provided by a real estate expert in your area.

Make sure these comps include any upgrades you've made to this point, especially any upgrades you can't see with the naked eye like insulation, wiring, and plumbing. There is also a ton of information about your home online. And your city hall will have zoning and tax information. Just don't fall into the trap that many homeowners do in thinking that the city tax assessment for your home is the actual market value. Sorry to say, it isn't. This is a value derived from looking at the average in the neighborhood. It doesn't take into account age and size of the home, nor its condition. Some municipalities give two values: a tax assessment and a value assessment. The

value assessment is closer to the market price; you may be relieved to learn that the tax assessment is often much lower (many people could not afford property tax on a full value assessment).

You should also do some digging when determining the purchase price of a home you are interested in buying—but we'll get to that later. A local real estate agent is your best bet for getting the most recent and accurate comps in your area. We talk more about home prices in the next chapter, so stay tuned.

JONATHAN: Under-pricing your property when you first list it is a better strategy to create excitement and enthusiasm among buyers and real estate agents than chasing the market. That's the phrase we use when homeowners continually lower their too-high price in order to entice buyers, often after the listing has already gone stale.

A listing is officially designated as new for two weeks on the Multiple Listing Service (MLS), the service real estate agents use to look for houses they may not personally represent. Most homes go

on the MLS because it offers the broadest opportunity for agents (and their buyers) to find properties, and it gives sellers the widest reach for buyers. The biggest benefit is that the MLS allows buyers to receive an auto email when properties that match their criteria are posted. It will only do this once for a new listing, so you want to make sure the house is priced to encourage viewings and offers. Fewer than 20 percent of our clients will want notifications of price reductions, so that first notification is key. Your house, with its appealing price, is sure to generate curiosity and showings.

Once the two-week period has passed, buyers may skip right over your house because it no longer comes up in an MLS search of "new listings." Even if you bring the price down, your listing is likely to be overlooked because as mentioned earlier, not all buyers get reduction notifications. Once your house has been on the market for a while and you keep reducing the price, it looks like you're desperate, and the only probable result will be lowball offers.

The dining room is all set for your buyer's next dinner party.

"REALTY" CHECK: THE FIVE PERCENT STRATEGY

One strategy to create interest in your house—and a potential bidding war—is to arrive at a price based on comps, and then set your price five percent below the average price. This generates a lot of traffic during the crucial first week on the market, and could lead to multiple offers, getting you a price well above asking and even above what the comps told you. With this strategy you need to ensure your home feels fresh and is staged well. There's no risk of being forced to sell for less than what you really want, and it is a strategy that experienced agents frequently engage in. It's legal in most states for sellers to reject a full-price offer, or any offer for that matter, except for reasons that are based on racial, ethnic, gender, or other illegal discrimination. The exception is that in certain states, sellers must accept a full-price, "clean" offer, or one that comes with no contingencies, such as the sale being conditional upon financing or on a home inspection. Those types of offers don't come along very often, and most buyers add contingencies into their offers anyway.

Stage a Great Sale

Here's the truth (and you might even be guilty of this on occasion): Most homebuyers have no imagination when looking at houses, so you have to do the thinking for them via strategic staging. *Staging* simply means adding or subtracting to the appearance of your house so it appeals to the widest possible array of needs and tastes. Staging creates the impression that life in your house is modern, tasteful, comfortable, organized, and, in short, fabulous. Buyers are distracted by personal stuff (which is why you cleaned house), rooms that aren't being used for their intended purpose (you're going to have to switch that snow globe collection room back into a bedroom, sorry!), and décor that does not match their taste (by now you must know the black and orange circus stripes in your dining room have to go). By staging a home well, you guide prospects through the features and assets of your home, show them how effectively the space can be used, and flaunt every square inch of potential your house has for the buyer.

Forget about *your* taste. You have to appeal to the majority of buyers, even though their specific preferences are unknown. Keep things somewhat neutral but never boring. Blend modern and classic, even if you live in a historic or "period" home. Take a minimalist approach, and choose furniture that is the right scale for the rooms. We've seen average sized master bedrooms (10 x 15 feet), for example, that are jammed with a king size bed topped with ten pillows, two nightstands, two dressers, and two chairs. It's too much. In a situation like this, you should remove one or both of the dressers and one of the chairs. Oh, and perhaps lose half the pillows.

A king size bed is beautifully dressed with a clean, crisp coverlet or quilt, two king-sized bed pillows, two standard-sized pillows, and an accent pillow. If possible, take a tip from television pros and consider getting brand new bedding for showings. Old clothes look old on camera; that's why a lot of TV pros have a set of new clothes to wear when on camera. That way the host looks polished and fresh. Keep your bedroom camera-ready while on the market with a brand new bedspread and pillows. Remember, you can take all the new stuff with you when you move.

In living areas, replace bulky and over-stuffed items with more streamlined silhouettes. Reconfigure the furniture placement so it's easy to flow through rooms. Do not put obstacles in the way of potential buyers. If they trip over a side table or fall over a chair, they will leave with a sore ankle and the idea that your house is way too small for their needs. If you do not have the confidence to arrange the rooms in your house on your own, hiring a professional

stager may help. Prices range broadly—from $500 to $5,000 and more—and depend on how much furniture they have to bring in and how long the house has to remain staged.

One huge benefit of using a professional home stager or staging/rental company is that you don't have the high costs of buying all the beautiful furniture and décor. An example: We've rented a $5,000 high-end modern couch for only a few hundred dollars. Grandma's old couch that you've held on to can't stand up to new modern pieces. If your home only needs staging for a couple of weeks, the price for the furniture rental will be substantially lower than if the house sits on the market for a few months or more. This is why it's so important to price your house well the first time.

Get rid of the visual clutter to show off your rooms.

Expand your counter space by
cleaning off everything but the
essentials.

STAGED

QUICK TIPS FROM STAGING PROS

1. **FOCUS.** Create a feature or a focal point in the living room so furniture is facing or arranged around something. This can mean either facing pieces toward a great view or away from a not-so-nice one. A fireplace, wall of art, or sleek flat-screen TV are great options to center furniture around. Play down a house that's too close to an industrial setting, or other unsightly features outside windows, by facing furniture away from these vistas.

2. **BE PURPOSEFUL.** Every room should have a purpose, and generally, it should reflect its intended purpose, especially if your house is square-footage challenged. Garages should be presented as a place to keep a car, not a pool table. Bedrooms should not be workout rooms.

3. **GO GREEN.** Bring in live plants to make the space feel fresh, and get rid of fake flower arrangements and dated "silk" plants. Be aware that some flowers like hydrangeas smell very foul when they start to turn, so stay on top of them and do a regular sniff check. Carnations, mums, alstroemeria flowers, and philodendron leaves are among the longest lasting cuttings. Be sure to take off any leaves on stems submerged in water (rotting leaves cause odor) and change the water every couple of days, always trimming the ends off slightly.

4. **RELAX.** The main purpose of living and family rooms is for leisure, so keep that in mind when choosing and arranging furniture. Make it look inviting and easy to sit down in. Arrange furniture to create areas of conversation, such as two sofas facing each other with a low coffee table in the middle.

5. **LIGHTEN UP.** If you can't install more recessed lighting, make sure shades are up to let natural light in, and place lamps strategically to brighten dark corners. Also put in the highest watt bulbs indicated on your fixtures.

6. **REMOVE THE BULK.** If your living room feels small, remove some furniture to create the illusion of space. If you have two couches, maybe swap one of them for two chairs.

7. **DEFINE IT.** Use area rugs to create separate spaces in large rooms.

8. **BE COMPULSIVE.** Since buyers snoop in drawers and closets, show them how organized their lives could be if they only lived in your house: alphabetize spice jars; stack dishes according to size; turn coffee cup handles facing the same way, or hang them in the same direction from cup hooks; organize clothes closets by type of clothes and color, i.e., hang shirts with shirts and pants with pants, going from light to dark; line up shoes. You wouldn't believe how far this perceived "pride of ownership" goes in reassuring buyers.

9. **BE FUNCTIONAL.** Small spaces can be made to look very practical with the careful use of storage ottomans, moveable islands, and multi-function furniture.

1: Architecturally interesting windows, or the view out of them, are a great focal point for any room.

2: Every room should have a purpose.

3: Small entryways only require a few well-chosen accessories.

1: The staging in this room helps show off the brick wall.

2: Throw open the drapes to let the sunshine in!

3: Some candles, greenery, and fruit are simple ways to dress up a dining room table if you don't want to (or can't) keep it set for dinner.

4: If you have glass cabinets, make sure what you see through them is organized and pretty.

5: Keep open shelves organized and airy.

3

4

5

Market Savvy

Real estate, like many other businesses, runs on the economics of supply and demand. You have to advertise properties in every way available. Find an agent who knows how to use the MLS, Craigslist, social media outlets, newspaper ads, virtual tours, contacting the real estate community, and, yes, a For Sale sign in front of your house.

Sure, we have clients who tell us they do not want a sign in front of their house. However, the more people who see your property, the better chance you have of selling fast for top dollar! When we use a For Sale sign on the front of a property, we light it with an LED system so it can be seen at night. We also place a pocket on our signs to hold brochures so passersby can take them.

We've even canvassed the community, talking to people and distributing brochures about our houses. Think about it: If your neighbors know your house is for sale, and one of their family/friends happens to want to relocate close to them, your house will be the first place that pops to mind. Everybody is always the biggest advocate for his or her own community. Your neighbor might say, "Hey, there's a house for sale on my street, and it's a great community."

Don't worry too much about holding an open house because these events rarely sell houses. Rather, they are an opportunity for your agent to find other clients, and for your neighbors to sneak a peek in your house. However, if your house has a feature that is so unique people have to see it in person, such as an unbelievable kitchen or an ultra-deluxe master suite that opens to a private garden, or is an important historic home with one-of-a-kind architectural details, an open house may make sense.

Consider getting professional photographs of your home's exterior and interior, and then using them to create a brochure—a detailed calling card for your house. When we create a house brochure, we include a map of the area with distances to amenities, including shopping, major highways, airports, schools, and so on. We also talk about all the things you can't see, including the fact that any new work was done with the proper permits, if there is a new roof and new windows, the R-value of windows, how efficient the heating system is, and so on. Aside from a detailed brochure, we also put small placards around the house to point out features and benefits buyers may miss—such as "tankless hot water system" on the door to the utility room. But don't go placard crazy: you don't need to label "This wall is blue" on a blue wall.

You may see mega-marketing as overkill, but we see it as smart. People who are searching for a home can look at 10 to 15 properties at a time. If you provide them with an extra-detailed brochure and many ways to access info about your house, they will remember your home long after they have forgotten all the others. We've sold more than one house this way. Don't be shy about talking up your house to anyone who will listen!

THE BOLD BUY

FIND THE HOUSE OF YOUR DREAMS

When Jonathan started our Las Vegas house hunt, he used a real estate agent to narrow down the search and choose properties that fit our criteria. We were new to the area (and not yet licensed in Nevada) and wanted a local market expert who could offer an opinion on what was available. A Realtor can, and should, be your ally in a home search, but ultimately, you are responsible for researching the facts about a home's location and its features: the community, common problems with houses in the area, local zoning, bylaws, tax assessments, crime rates, amenities, schools, and so on. Bottom line: *Know a neighborhood before you designate it as your target.* Don't waste time looking in an area that doesn't suit your needs. Location is key because that's the one thing you can't change.

Your real estate agent is somewhat limited in what they can and can't do for you. In fact, in most jurisdictions it's illegal for real estate professionals to engage in what's called *steering,* or the act of discouraging buyers from looking in a particular neighborhood that may be considered "bad" for any reason at all.

The fines and penalties are quite extreme for real estate agents who break these laws. So, it is important to understand what you want and pay attention to the facts about a community. If you're concerned about crime in a neighborhood, there are city websites with statistics on crime. If you only want to live in a guard-gated, master-planned community … well, that will definitely narrow your search. A good real estate professional should be able to anticipate your needs and get you any answer, but sometimes you need to ask the right questions.

We had spent a lot of time in Las Vegas over the years and we knew the areas and kind of home we wanted. If we don't know an area well, we always do our own research and ask local real estate agents. We especially want to know about crime data and the quality of schools (generally speaking, the better the school, the more stable the community). These are two areas that are key for most homebuyers. Demographic information comes in handy if you're looking for a certain lifestyle. For instance if you're single and want to meet people, a community where 68 percent of the people are married with kids might not be the best choice. On the other hand, if you're retired and looking for cultural opportunities, a myriad of dining options, and an interesting jazz scene, you'll probably want to avoid college neighborhoods, which tend to be all about cheap, watered-down beer and loud rock music.

The internet makes exploration easier than ever. Check out websites such as city-data.com, census.gov, fbi.gov (search for "crime statistics"), and greatschools.com are helpful in gathering facts about an area, including the ratio of men to women, median age, people with college educations, political affiliations, and levels of income. When looking to invest in a neighborhood we are not familiar with, tools like these can give us a snapshot of an area. But nothing beats actually spending time in a community to find out what it's like during the day, at night, on weekends, and seasonally.

We looked at one house that turned out to have a commuter train in the backyard, which ran through very early in the morning and during the evening—and it was loud. The whole house shook. Some urban communities may have nightclubs that are only active in the evening hours but can produce a lot of noise, unruly customers and crime. All the street parking can dry up, and you'll see people from other neighborhoods roaming around, making noise.

"NEEDS TLC" AND
Other Real Estate Code Words

We've all heard it—the hyperbole real estate agents use to describe a home that makes fatal flaws sound like fantastic features. Some real estate agents may try, through deceptive wordplay, to paint rosy pictures of places that are clearly not the right fit for you. "Untouched beauty," "diamond in the rough," and "handyman special" are generic terms that don't describe the actual house but are meant to give you a positive impression so that when you see the place with your own eyes, you won't be deterred by obvious shortcomings.

Freakonomics: A Rogue Economist Explores the Hidden Side of Everything, by Steven D. Levitt and Stephen J. Dubner, analyzes the words real estate agents use to entice buyers. They found that the highest sale prices correlate with actual physical descriptions of the home itself: very specific terms such as *granite*, *Corian*, *walnut*, *marble*, *crown molding*, *stainless steel*, *gourmet*, *state-of-the-art*, *energy efficient*, and so on. These are more useful than more general descriptors when evaluating the condition and style of a house before you've seen it.

Sometimes, positive sounding phrases correlate to a less desirable house. For instance, Levitt and Dubner contend that when a house is listed as *well-maintained,* it is subtly encouraging you to make a lower offer, because well maintained means it's an older house that needs updating. We've found their theory to be true, so if you are in the market for a fixer and want to renovate, a *well-maintained* home may be just what you're looking for. You see, even the most generic terms actually do have meaning; they are code words for specific issues in a house that you want to be aware of before making an appointment to step inside its door. Turn the page for our cheat sheet on agent-speak; it's especially helpful when these words are not accompanied by anything specific.

ARTISTIC: Weird paint colors on walls, DIY mosaic floors, or odd backsplashes that will have to be removed immediately.

CHARMING: Has strange quirks and a weird layout, lots of small rooms, none of which may work for modern lifestyles. Can also mean small.

CLASSIC: Dated.

COZY: Small. Make that tiny.

FANTASTIC: Not fantastic. Agent wants to move it off the market as quickly as possible.

FURNISHED: Sellers don't want to move their stuff so the buyer must get rid of it.

GREAT NEIGHBORHOOD: This house may not be that nice, but the area is good. It's the worst house in the best neighborhood. This isn't necessarily a bad thing. We look for these opportunities!

HISTORIC: May need updates including new wiring and plumbing. Can also indicate that renovations will cost much more as historic district rules might dictate that specific materials and methods must be used. Approvals can take much longer for historic properties if they are registered historic houses or are located in a registered historic neighborhood. Your real estate agent should have these details.

LOTS OF POTENTIAL: Needs a complete overhaul.

NATURAL LANDSCAPING: No landscaping, weeds, and a deer problem—you can't grow anything.

NEAR SHOPPING OR CONVENIENT TO AMENITIES: On a busy street.

NEEDS TLC: Total gut job. Maybe even a teardown.

NEEDS UPDATING: The kitchen, every bathroom, and all the carpeting need to be replaced.

NEW ROOF: Everything else is old.

PRESTIGIOUS: Overpriced.

PRIME LOCATION: Could be a teardown.

RECENTLY PAINTED: And that's about it.

SEASONAL STREAM BORDERS PROPERTY: Next to storm culvert, flooding potential.

SOLD AS-IS: Seller will not do any repairs and may know of issues they are not disclosing.

SPACIOUS: May not be large, but has an open feel. Could be decrepit and impractical.

THIS ONE WON'T LAST LONG: Overpriced and looking for an out of state buyer.

UPDATED BATHROOM: Kitchen needs work.

UPDATED KITCHEN: New countertops, cabinets have been painted, new but mid- or low-range appliances; bathrooms need updating.

Every style of house, from 1970s ranches to 1920s traditional homes, have unique charm. Give them all a chance.

Core Comp Concepts

When scouting a neighborhood, be skeptical when residents mention recent selling prices, which in our experience, they often do. Homeowners can't resist volunteering inflated sales figures of the homes around them because they want their own homes to be worth more than they are. Who doesn't? This is where real estate agents come in—yours can and should run a comparative market analysis (a CMA or *comp*), which shows the actual sales prices of comparable homes in your area or in the area where you want to buy. In-depth comps, or *comparables*, are one of the best tools for determining a home's value. They analyze recently sold properties in a neighborhood similar to the one you are looking at and comparable to the house according to age, size, livable square footage, lot size, and features and finishes. Keep in mind that a proper, detailed comp takes hours to prepare and involves a detailed analysis of at least the closest five matching houses.

When you look at the comps your agent provides, you might see some houses that seem similar to one another, however one has sold for $50,000 more. Don't simply focus on the selling price—dig deeper into the report. Two houses can look exactly the same, but the house that sold for $50,000 more may have come with a built-in stereo system, luxury

landscaping, or a boat. That's right … a listed sale price can include anything from a hot tub or 14K-gold-plated toilet to a car or rare art. You would never know this by just looking at a list of prices for all the sold homes in an area. Discrepancies like these may not always make it to generic reports, so this is where an agent comes in. Your agent can pull detailed listing information or contact colleagues to reveal special items that may have been included in the sale of the house. We saw comps of one lakefront property that showed a house that sold for more than another even though the livable or finished square footage, lot size, lake frontage, and house style (colonial) were nearly identical. What made the $30,000 difference in price? The more expensive house came with two canoes, a kayak, a large dock, outdoor furniture, and extensive backyard landscaping. This happens way more than you think.

If you plan on buying a fixer-upper that needs major work, you want to make sure you're offering the right price, so the CMA you use to arrive at an offer price should take into consideration how the current state of the property compares to other similar homes in the area. However, to ensure the house is worth all the work you plan to put into it, you'll also want to ask the agent for a CMA of houses that are comparable to your house once your theoretical renovations are completed. This comp will give you a good idea of how much you can spend on a reno without making a bad investment. If it doesn't look like you could get everything you need in the renovated house without overspending, then it's not the right house. Always, always think of resale even if you *think* this will be your forever home.

Other questions a good CMA can answer are: How long do fixer-uppers sit on the market in desirable neighborhoods? Are resale houses in different areas selling at the same pace? Have sale prices generally gone up or down over the past six to nine months? How high or low is the resale inventory in the city? This will determine if it's a buyer's market or a seller's market. What features did those houses that sold faster have, and what was wrong with the houses that sat on the market longer? Was it price alone, location, or condition?

"REALTY" CHECK: HOW MUCH HOUSE CAN YOU AFFORD?

Don't spend too much time (if any) looking at houses outside of your total maximum budget, including renovation costs, because if you fall in love with a house you can't afford, you will be frustrated by all those less expensive homes that can't possibly match up. One of the tricks Drew loves to play on buyers on *Property Brothers* is starting the home search by bringing them to a turnkey, move-in ready house, packed with all their must-haves and didn't-even-know-I-wanted items. When they find out the price, which is always a budget buster, and get over the urge to strangle Drew, they understand why we advocate looking at fixers that can get all their must-haves within their reno budget.

We're not bankers, but we've bought enough properties to know the rule of thumb about figuring out what you can afford. Monthly payments for a home should generally not exceed 28 percent of your gross monthly income. Calculate a mortgage payment for houses in your price range, and add any additional expenses such as taxes, insurance, utilities, and maintenance. (Mortgage calculators are easily found on the web.) If you plan on making changes in the house, factor that in by combining your max budget for a fixer-upper, plus the cost of upgrades you want to make to get your final number. Talk with your lender to see what your options are. Depending on the product, your credit, and the down payment, you can sometimes negotiate a better rate and therefore lower monthly payment.

BROTHER VS. BROTHER:

Common Buying Blunders

DREW: Let's get one thing clear—buying a house is not like speed dating. A mistake many buyers make is forgetting that beauty or ugliness is only skin deep. A house can be made to appear attractive during a quick walkthrough, but is the veneer of beauty worth the premium price? People often base value on attractiveness. In real estate that approach can burn you because the ugly duckling can oftentimes be a swan with cosmetic changes and repairs, while the beautiful-looking place might be a facade that's hiding some scary, expensive-to-fix issues. The diamond in the rough property could be your true love, if you give it a chance. I like to meet with clients in their current home, take them from room to room, and ask them to point out some specifics that explain why they are moving from the house. Then we figure out together how much house (plus renovation costs) they can afford. We always want to make sure that what they are searching for won't make them house rich and pocket poor.

JONATHAN: Another blunder is becoming so infatuated with a house that you forget about the neighborhood. It can be very easy to say, "I absolutely love the kitchen (or the bathroom or the closets), so I'll ignore the salvage yard next door or the fact that a train runs by and shakes the house every 30 minutes." Don't gloss over unchangeable facts. By purchasing a home with built-in, permanent negatives, you drastically reduce the number of future buyers you may be able to sell it to unless you get it so cheaply that a resale profit is guaranteed—a next-to-impossible feat.

Just because you're willing to settle for a major inconvenience (and are you really?) doesn't mean that others will settle for the same headache. Are you willing to put up with the issue for the next ten years, or will it wear thin on you too? So that head-over-heels fabulous kitchen could cost you a heck of a lot more when you eventually sell. You could have found a home with more potential in a much better location for a better price because it needed an update. It costs a lot less to put in a beautiful new kitchen than to try to sell a home in an undesirable location. It's a mistake to be so emotional or desperate to buy that you ignore red flags or compromise on your budget. Trust me, you can always find another house. It's hard to recover from a bad financial decision of this magnitude.

DREW: The second mistake that buyers make is not being able to see beyond the ugly. Sometimes a house is priced really low because it's extremely out of date in

terms of kitchens, baths, shag carpeting, vinyl floorings, wall colors, and so on but the cost of the updates is well worth it due to the home's location, original features, size, or structural condition. Have some imagination and look at the bones of a house and the possibilities. Look past, beyond, under, and over all the clutter and personal décor decisions when looking at a house. You could get a killer deal on a great property simply because most other buyers think that the dirty purple shag rug in the family room or hideous fixtures in the bathrooms somehow define the house. They don't. Flaws like that are relatively inexpensive to change. Perhaps you can just refinish or repaint a built-in at a minimal cost and make it look brand new. Look at the yard space, not the neon plastic toys sitting in it! Focus your attention on important existing value items like hardwood floors in good condition, crown molding, ample-sized rooms, good overall proportions—the characteristics of a house that make it a good prospect.

JONATHAN: I agree with Drew about looking past the owner's personal taste, but you also have to understand that if the structure of a house isn't good, "Money Pit" will become a reality and not just a cliché (or the title of a Tom Hanks classic). The third mistake people make is not understanding that structural integrity is the foundation of what you can and can't do to a house, and frankly, whether or not you should even attempt a renovation. If you get a house at the right price, changes like reconfiguring a floor plan or adding a bathroom (or two) can fit into your overall budget, but only if the structure is good. Almost anything can be done to a well-built house. But a lousy structure? That can eat up your budget faster than anything else. We once walked away from a house that needed so much foundation work and a complete structural overhaul that no matter how much work we put into it, it would never be worth what we put in. In that case, it didn't matter how great the location—if we bought it at $600,000 and put in another

$400,000 to fix it, we would have been in the red until our future grandkids were in college, and probably longer.

DREW: There's a fine point where no renovation will ever make it a good investment. It'll just cost too much to fix. The only option in this scenario is tearing it down. That's not to say that a teardown (a property that would cost more to rehab than to take down to build now) is a bad thing, and we've had many clients who have made a lot of money doing this. You just have to ensure that the properties are in neighborhoods where land is valuable, like beachfront communities and neighborhoods that are quickly gentrifying.

It's just that the average buyer can't afford to front the cash for the construction of a whole new home. Most of the time, people are buying houses they do not plan to bulldoze. So run the math on all worst-case scenarios, and do not over-leverage yourself. Most of the time we've found the best investment is the one where you can purchase it at a good price, salvage much of the existing building, and just correct the problems and aesthetic. Save the teardowns for when you've got the entire cost of the land purchase and build sitting in cash burning a hole in your pocket.

JONATHAN: I have to add the fourth and fifth mistakes (besides, I like to have the last word). A house that is a bit beyond budget, say less than 3 percent over, can often be negotiated down to suit your finances. So go ahead and take a look at houses that are beyond your max budget, but make it a rule that you'll never pay more for a house than it is worth. Finally, never look at a house as the final one you'll ever buy. In most cases, there is really no such thing as a "forever house."

It used to be that a couple purchased a home and it was kept in the family for generations. Well, now the average person moves every five years. So always look at a possible purchase in terms of its potential resale value—even if that day is 20 years from now.

Two houses, two different values. The one above is very snazzy—it's 2,500 square feet and has two master bedrooms, central air conditioning, and hardwood floors throughout, plus a modern kitchen with all the bells and whistles. The three bathrooms are spa-like. It sits on an ample one-third-acre lot with nice landscaping. The house on the left looks a bit neglected. It's crying out for a paint job and some of the shrubbery needs to be trimmed. The inside, all 1,800 square feet of it, has some nice original features like crown molding and wide-plank, white-pine floors, but it needs repainting and refinishing. The bathroom (there's just one) and the kitchen are both badly dated and in need of replacing. The porch is sagging.

Which is more valuable? The house on the left of course! It's right downtown in a very lively and desirable neighborhood and close to shopping, schools, restaurants, and other amenities. The house above is nice, but it's in the suburbs, far from many attractions and things to do. The smaller downtown house, on the left, is actually worth more, and it's a better buy. Once it's fixed up, you'll have a lot of equity for your investment. If you change your mind and don't want to live in it, you could turn around and sell it and make a profit. You simply can't tell the value of a home just by looking at it out of context.

Be a Critical Shopper

It's a lot of fun to look at houses, at least in the beginning of a search when the anticipation of finding that magical place where you will make memories and enjoy friends and family still feels fresh and exciting. But like we said earlier, the biggest investment in your life (that's buying a house for most people) has to be done less with your heart and more with your mind. Of course you have to get a good vibe from a house, but you can't let emotions run your life or your house-buying strategy. That's why we, along with most real estate pros, recommend making an offer on a house based solely on facts and contingent on an acceptable home inspection.

You are in the best position to make decisions on a property *before* you buy it. At this early stage you can always back out of a deal if the results don't meet your expectations, which is why an inspection is a recommended contingency when buying a home. Generally, the home inspector is brought in soon after the offer is accepted. Once you close the deal, it's a lot harder to get your money back or complain about any issues. About 95 percent of all house sales are subject to a home inspection today, according to the American Society of Home Inspectors. For comparison, in 1994 only 75 percent of homes were inspected before purchase.

Another advantage to making an offer subject to inspection is that you can tie up the property while you're dotting all your I's and crossing all your T's and prevent somebody else from waltzing in and taking it. Just remember that asking for a home inspection does weaken your offer a little, as the buyer sees this as an opportunity to say you don't like something and may want to reduce the price or walk away. So only ask for a home inspection if you really intend on getting one.

Understand that usually the effectiveness of a home inspection is limited to the most common issues and the areas that are currently open to view. However, there are other options for conditions to an offer. For example, if you're buying a place you know needs a major renovation or very specific work, make the offer subject to a bid or quote from a licensed contractor on the work that needs to be done. Wouldn't it be smart to get your contractor to give you a written estimate on the work you want done before you actually purchase the property? That way you get to see if your numbers still make sense. Keep in mind too that a licensed general contractor (or sub trade if the work needed is specific) likely has much more experience and education than your average home inspector. Regardless, never rely solely on the information provided by any of these inspections. You are the potential owner, and you need to make sure you're comfortable with everything. The more information you have upfront, the better position you are in to make an accurate offer that leaves you in good financial shape to make the necessary changes. Or you can walk away from a house if it looks like what you want to do won't be cost effective when added to the purchase price.

If you're hesitant to spend the money on an inspection, don't be. It's a good investment —and normally one that costs between $400 and $500 for a typical 2,000-square-foot house, which in the scheme of things isn't that much considering how much money it could save you in the long run. Sure, there are numerous home inspection apps on the market, but most are targeted toward professional home inspectors. Some general inspection apps are created for homebuyers, which provide useful checklists. However, there are some aspects of a home's construction and infrastructure (electrical wiring, plumbing, heating and cooling systems, roof construction, and so on) that require a pro to inspect. Do you really know what you're looking at when you peek into a junction box or examine the waste line of a sewer system? Drew can peer into a closet and tell immediately if it's large enough to hold all his shirts, shoes, and belts, while Jonathan can look at an HVAC system and know if it's going to make it through another frigid winter or boiling summer. Both are important.

A home inspector's report reviews the condition of the home's heating and cooling systems, plumbing and electrical systems, the roof, attic, visible insulation, walls, ceilings, floors, windows, doors, foundation, basement, and any other visible structures. Most inspectors also offer additional services not included in the price of a typical home inspection. If you are worried about environmental aspect of the home, you can request mold, radon, and water testing at an additional cost (from $50 per test), as well as thermal imagery that measures heat and air loss, inspections typically known as energy audits (from $300 for a small house to more than $600 for a large home over 3,000 square feet).

One of the aspects of home inspection that bothers us as buyers (and we keep this in mind as sellers too) is that a home inspection often results in a long list of items that need repair, when in reality many are typical wear and tear in a used home and the seller shouldn't be required to fix them. So do not expect the seller to take care of every last thing on that list, and do not expect everything on the list to automatically lower the price of the house. Just keep in mind that some sellers may feel they have already accounted for the work that needs to be done and won't be willing to adjust the price further. This is fine because you are a savvy buyer who is not going to overpay for a house anyway. You'll find a place where the seller is being realistic … or where the numbers make better sense.

While the inspection process is going on, be sure to visit the house at different times of day and on different days of the week. This is especially necessary if the listing says "by appointment only," or showings are limited to specific times and days. Also, don't just drive by; walk around and talk to the locals who can provide a lot of valuable insight and insider tips.

The main value of speaking with neighbors is to identify any red flags. Locals will give you the dirt on a town's pros and cons in a heartbeat, and that includes the behavior of the previous occupants of the house you're considering. People have made us aware of houses used for drug manufacturing, past and recent unpermitted work, rowdy nearby clubs, and massive overnight parking shortages. These are all things our clients wouldn't have known just from reading the listing—or even doing a cursory walkthrough of the house with a real estate agent. Don't think that just cleaning up visible evidence of a former pot growing operation is enough—drug manufacturing presents all sorts of health issues, and such houses may not be fit for habitation without serious remediation. From mold and toxins to illegal wiring and even unwanted visits from "customers" at all hours of the day and night, there's a lot more to one of these houses than meets the eye.

For example, if a neighbor says the last inhabitants of a property were party animals, or there was a great number of people coming and going, you should look for signs of a former drug operation including signs of damage cover-up. This is much more common than you may think. When we were buying and selling full time we found, in one year, four marijuana grow houses. Some of the signs: large holes cut in walls that have been patched; shady looking electrical work; a telltale musty smell; furniture placed in odd configurations to hide holes in walls; water stains on walls, and, of course, plant remnants. Jonathan once found harvested and dead pot plants in a home's crawl space.

Even freshly painted rooms might be a red flag. Usually, new paint just means the homeowners have repainted the wall to make the house show better. But there are times

Check out the traffic and parking situation during peak commuting times. While it could be tough to nab a parking spot, a busy area also indicates activity and safety.

it can be covering up evidence of a fire or leak. Anytime a house looks newly renovated, don't automatically assume all is well. Ask for a renovation breakdown or report, and make sure all necessary permits were pulled, i.e., all plumbing, electrical, drywall, and structural jobs were inspected and approved. Get the Certificate of Occupancy, or CO, from the previous owner. It will detail any problems that needed to be corrected after a major renovation was completed. If the seller no longer has it … another red flag. You can always check with the city to see if they have a copy on file.

Look out for indications that no permits were pulled for renovation work. We looked at one house with a staircase that had spindles on the interior stair railing that were spaced about 10 inches apart. Legally spindles can be no more than 4 inches apart, so this was clearly a violation. No way would an inspector approve such a staircase. This made us look into other possible violations that weren't so readily visible, and we found both plumbing and electrical issues in the house, which we ultimately advised our clients not to buy, unless the value of those repairs were taken into consideration and a thorough home inspection was done. A home like this where the seller has done a lot of unpermitted work can be like opening Pandora's box. There can easily be thousands of dollars in hidden problems.

Ultimately, you must consider the value of a home in its current condition. The value of the house is always based on the whole picture of what you are getting: condition, features, location, size, and lot. Some houses are priced to sell quickly so there's no more wiggle room in the price. One of those pot grow houses we told you about earlier was listed at a rock bottom price because the seller knew what her renters had done to it. In order to get it sold but still turn a profit she demanded a minimum price that we just couldn't make work. In the end, we passed and found another property that offered even more opportunity. Which isn't all that unusual: any time we think we've found an amazing property and it doesn't work out, we always seem to find something even better.

MONEY ON THE TABLE:
Your Offer

Putting in an offer on a house is a thrill no matter how many times we've done it. We've bought a lot of houses, and the anticipation about whether or not our offer will be accepted is always there. The excitement of the moment when a seller says "yes" never fades. We can't imagine getting jaded by the real estate business—it's too much fun, and it's too lucrative for us to ever take it for granted.

There is more than one way to buy a house. Remember, we bought our first house with very little money down. One of the most common ways to buy a property with little or no money down is to use owner financing, also called *vendor take-back* or *seller carry-back*. The current owner of the house agrees to finance either all or some part of the purchase price. Instead of getting the cash now, they are willing to receive an income stream in the form of your monthly payments under the terms you both agree on. The seller is acting as a bank, and rather than receiving all the monies at closing, they "lend" the money to the buyers by letting them pay for the house via regular payments, which may just represent the principal or the purchase price only, or the principal plus interest. You might be surprised to know that many people who own their properties free and clear (no longer carry a mortgage on it) are willing to finance the entire amount or a good portion of the mortgage at great terms. Because vendor take-back mortgages are convenient, be prepared for them to have a slightly higher interest rate.

This sort of financial gymnastics is becoming more common in North America; in a difficult housing market, people who want to get rid of a property are often more willing to be creative. Assuming a homeowner's mortgage is another strategy you can use in some rare instances. It means you take over ownership of a homeowner's property without going through the process of a formal sale. The buyer often pays the seller a cash deposit, which can be much less than a conventional down payment of 20 percent of the purchase price. After that, the seller transfers his mortgage title over to the buyer, making the buyer the new legal owner of the property. The buyer then has to make the mortgage payments.

Today, very few mortgages in the U.S. are assumable (it's a much more common practice in Europe). Government-backed mortgages, such as FHA and VA loans, are assumable if the buyer meets certain qualifications. Mortgages on these houses present a buying opportunity for you because it may be easier for you to assume a mortgage than get one on your own, depending on your own financial picture. Mostly, however, mortgage

PREVIOUS PAGE, THIS PAGE & NEXT PAGES: What makes you fall in love with a house? It could be anything: a beautiful, defined entryway; fabulous kitchen; space for a home office; enough bedrooms to make all the kids happy; room for a man cave; or a hobby room.

assumptions present risks for banks since it's difficult for bankers to sufficiently evaluate the person taking over the mortgage. The mortgage you may be trying to take over was assumed for the individual you are buying the house from; it was not approved for you and your individual financial picture. Even more, banks don't like assumable mortgages because they lose out on the money made from closing costs and interest charges related to new mortgages.

Whether you want to try some creative and nonconventional ways to finance the purchase of your house or if you want to go the conventional route and apply for a mortgage, you need to find an agent who is aligned with what you are trying to do—and who has the knowledge and skills to help you accomplish your goals. Just understand that there are options, and you need to familiarize yourself with what those may be. You may even be eligible for government grants or preferred rates on financing, so don't have the tunnel vision view that there is only one way to get into real estate.

Make sure your expectations are realistic. Everyone wants a "deal." Well, in our minds, a "deal" is not overpaying for a property but paying market value and enjoying the house. A "deal" is not wasting your time seeing properties that are completely beyond your means. When shopping for a house, you are in a situation where you want to buy a commodity for the lowest price possible and the seller wants to sell it for the highest price possible. Those are opposing desires and you have to find a way to balance them out so everybody gets what they want.

Once again, it's all about the comps. People often complain to us that they put in offer after offer on houses, and they continually get rejected or beaten out by other buyers. Say a house is worth $800,000 (the comps will tell you that), and it is listed at $750,000. Your agent should explain to you that the house is being priced lower than market value to generate multiple offers, which in most cases works. If a house is listed $50,000 below market value, then why put in an offer lower than that, or even at the asking price for that matter? Yet, people do it all the time, and they lose houses that way. It's better to beat out the other buyers with a stronger offer closer to market value. It's a mistake to make a really low-ball offer on a house. It can insult the seller, who won't even want to make a counter offer at that point. Every offer should be based on several variables:

> Comps (or comparables)—the price at which similar houses in similar neighborhoods sold for in the last three to six months: Markets can change rapidly, so what a house sold for one year ago is not a good comparison.

> Existing problems the house may have, which the seller is not willing to fix: You have to subtract the amount of money it will take to fix those problems from your offer price—and explain that to the seller.

> How long the house has been sitting on the market: The longer a house sits, the more negotiating room you have to make a lower offer.

> Whether there are other offers on the table: The more offers you're competing with, the less of a margin you have to reduce the purchase price.

Conditions on offers are very common when purchasing real estate, but they do weaken an offer. Either the buyer or the seller can put a condition on for literally anything, and we've seen some strange ones, as in, "Condition to our goldfish liking the house." The most common ones you see in offers are subject to a buyer's conditions, including a home inspection and financing. However, if you're in a competitive situation, you can strengthen your offer by removing all conditions and making a "clean" offer.

This can be a great, strategic way to have your offer accepted, but there are risks. Are you comfortable not having a home inspection? There could be lots of hidden problems. Even though you're approved for financing, the lending bank still needs to approve the house. What if they don't value it at the purchase price? Will you be able to make up the difference? We often make a long list of needed repairs and work the cost of repair into the offer. Finally, if possible, be flexible with the closing date so you can appeal to the seller's needs.

One more strategy you can use is the emotional tug letter. Sometimes it works, and sometimes it doesn't. Since it doesn't cost a thing, it's worth a shot. Say a young couple wants to start a family. Writing a letter to the owner telling them how much they love the house and how they will care for it and bring their children up in it can have a profound effect on homeowners who have been in their house for a long time and cherish it.

In the same way, there may be a benefit in telling the story of the buyer. Our clients were interested in a house, in a great neighborhood, that a family had owned for 60 years. The sellers had priced it slightly below market value, so they received multiple officers, including our clients'. One offer was from an investor, one was from a single person, and one was from a family—our clients. The family got the house, even though their offer was $20,000 less than the investor's offer, because Drew sold the story to the owners that this nice family wanted to raise their family there. He convinced them that our clients appreciated the history and value of the house while the investor just wanted to flip it.

THE PROS
HAVE IT

WHY HIRING EXPERTS SAVES MONEY, TIME … AND YOUR RELATIONSHIPS

On *Property Brothers,* we generally start work on a project as quickly as possible, the moment the ink dries on the contract, because we're working with incredibly short timelines. But you have to keep in mind that we've been renovating houses since the mid '90s. We've seen it all! Within five minutes of walking into a house, we can picture the best possible layout and design for the space. If you don't have that same eye for transforming a home, there is a happy medium, and in fact, there are many benefits to living in a house for a short while before you call in the wrecking crews. We know you're anxious to get going on those renovations you've been dreaming about ever since you fell in love with the possibilities for that '70s-era avocado-green kitchen and pink tile bathroom. It can pay dividends to live in a space for a while, even if it's just a few months, to get a feel for how you move and function once you're unpacked. When you understand how you might best use the space on an experiential level, your renovation is more likely to reflect how you truly want to live.

Don't trick
yourself into
thinking you
are capable of
doing more
than you can.

    Besides, you have to have a plan. Part of that plan must include professionals. The pros make things easier for you. We offer guarantees, and we have insurance if things go wrong. But most importantly … we know what we're doing. We're all for DIY, and we love it when homeowners lend a hand and put in some sweat equity to lower costs. They learn about their house in the process and even pick up some skills that are handy for homeowners to know. (See our list of reno jobs you might want to DIY at the end of the chapter.) But for best results the fact is, unless you're super skilled in finishing carpentry, plumbing, and electrical, if you want your home renovation to look good, use the pros.

Here are a few examples of what can go comically wrong when homeowners decide to tackle home reno projects themselves— or get talked into hiring their "very talented" brother-in-law's second cousin once removed. While friends and family are great for painting parties, helping move debris or furniture, and other household chores, only let experienced professionals assist with actual renovations.

IT'S NOT THAT WE DON'T WANT
You to Get Your Hands Dirty ...

We are not opposed to amateur homeowners tackling big renovation jobs, but you have to be realistic. Do you know the first thing about being a general contractor? And don't you already have a full-time job? Nothing causes a construction budget to elevate faster than an unorganized general contractor and delays. You're likely going to have some sort of learning curve at your "new" full-time job as a GC—make no mistake, renovating a house is all-consuming. The project may go slowly and create even more stress on your already busy life. And you may not enjoy the work either. Installing cabinetry, rebuilding stairs, and installing light fixtures may seem like fun if you've seen it done on television: Every project looks easier when it's all wrapped up neatly in 60 minutes. That's just not reality, and the long timelines can wear on your patience. So all we recommend, and we've said it many times, is that you be honest with yourself. Do you really have the desire to do this work? How about time—have you got enough? And what about skills?

Yes, we've read the numerous blog posts written by enthusiastic DIYers who have redone their Victorian mansions in a span as little as three months. It's true that some people have a natural affinity for construction and building, and that's why they brag about their skills on a blog. But what about the thousands of other people who don't have a natural gift for using a hammer and nails, for taking accurate measurements, or for picking the right materials? No, we're not talking about Drew! (He'll kick Jonathan's butt for saying that.) Professional contractors and tradespeople are often the best option for ensuring a renovation turns out as you hoped.

Realize that on *Property Brothers* we are only finishing those three to four rooms you see within that six-week (depending on the project) timeline. We typically renovate the whole house, but there is a separate budget and separate renovation timeline for the other areas. And to add to that, if Jonathan (or other contractors) were doing the project outside of the show, work on those three or four rooms would be on closer to a 12-week timeline, which means if you were doing it on your own it would likely be about 24 weeks. Just know what you're getting into if you insist upon tackling major projects on your own or with a friend or spouse. (P.S.: There are a lot of reasons why many relationships do not survive a renovation. The longer it takes and the more it costs, the harder it's going to be not to fight. I don't care what your spouse says ... renovating your kitchen should *never* take two years!)

Aside from lacking the know-how to pull off a big project, the average person doesn't know how to value their time. You have a day job, and you're trying to mud, tile, and drywall your basement every evening to save $2,000? Is that really worth it? This might take you two weeks or more, and cause a lot of misery and exhaustion—not to mention potential time- and money-wasting mistakes. Trust us. That uneven tile you installed yourself will drive you nuts every time you look at it. A pro can do the same work in five days or less, during the day, when he's out of your hair, and do it well. That is *your* time you are saving. Change the thought process—put more value on your time and peace of mind. People are often afraid of contractors because of the cost involved, but the cost of mediocre DIY work is very high. Resale might be tougher or more expensive after you take on the improvements yourself— you're going to have to clean up those mistakes before you put the house on the market, often by hiring the pros you should have brought on in the first place.

Likewise, think twice about being the general contractor on a project. It comes down to your time, your organizational skills, and your knowledge. A good general contractor is worth paying for because he keeps a project on schedule, on track, and has all the contacts when someone calls in sick. If you answer the following questions with more nos than yeses, hire a general contractor:

> Do you know what permit and plans you will have to submit for the job?

_____

> Do you know which sub-contractors are necessary to complete your job?

_____

> Do you know which subs show up first on your job?

_____

> Do you know what to do if the painter doesn't show up? Can you quickly call another one who will come?

_____

> Are you able to accurately estimate all costs involved in a project so that you can properly budget in advance?

_____

> Can you answer subs' questions when they come to you with technical issues?

_____

> Can you make quick decisions on important matters so work can continue?

_____

> Can you judge the work subs are doing to make sure it is done correctly and to code?

_____

* Remember, this list doesn't even include the design side of your project, which is a whole other beast, which is covered in Chapter 7 (Feathering Your Nest, page 237).

BROTHER VS. BROTHER:

Hiring and Working with the Pros

JONATHAN: There are good and bad eggs in every profession. Deciding on a general contractor is a time when you should do a gut check. Go with your instincts as well as your intellect. Yes, of course you need to get references and follow up with them (keeping in mind a contractor is going to give you the names and numbers of his best customers), but if a contractor or any kind of professional makes you feel like an idiot for asking questions, doesn't seem forthcoming, or talks to you in overly complex ways that you can't understand, find someone else. Likewise, if you don't get a call back from a contractor within 24 hours, cross the company off your list. That's a serious red flag!

Non-responsiveness before a job indicates they might not be responsive once they start the job.

DREW: Jonathan didn't call me back once for 24 hours, but I let it pass since he wasn't working for me at the time. But I agree, don't hire any contractor who doesn't communicate promptly and professionally. We look for contractors who are in the business *as a career,* not a part-time hobby. That might mean passing on your brother-in-law who does construction "on the side" in favor of a person who has an established business. That is generally someone who has an informational website, has business cards and marketing materials, preferably is on social media, shows they are organized, and is conscious of their reputation and image. Do they provide warranties on their work? Fly-by-night people generally don't.

JONATHAN: After you've found contractors with the qualities Drew mentioned,

get detailed quotes on the work from at least three of them, and get them in writing. Don't necessarily hire the contractor with the least expensive quote, and don't discount the contractor with the highest quote. Look at what they are promising to do, and ask to see the work they have already done. There are contractors who focus on decks, others who mainly do bathrooms, and some who only have experience building garages. If your renovation has several areas, meaning kitchen, bathroom, roofing, mechanical, or even landscaping, be sure the contractor you hire has done *all* of the types of work before. You don't need to pay somebody to learn on the job.

DREW: Just as you have to ensure any and all contractors and trades are properly credentialed and licensed (if and when necessary), make sure all general contractors you're interested in hiring have insurance, which protects them and your job in case

of accident or theft. Your home insurance company may also want you to add a rider during the renovation, so call them to find out what they require before signing a contract and allowing work to start. The last thing you need is to find out you didn't have the proper coverage *after* something happens. Bonded contractors can ask for and receive a deposit upfront. The same is true if the contractor is affiliated with a professional homebuilder program (there are several national programs where they insure the contractor, such as the National Association of Home Builders). But know that a large number of contractors who ask for big deposits up front are not legally allowed to do so—call your municipality and professional organizations before writing a check.

JONATHAN: In fact, never put down a deposit on work until you have a written agreement that stipulates in detail what work they will do and when, and how much it will cost. It should also stipulate what happens with the deposit should

either party not fulfill the agreement. Many contractors will give you a breakdown of costs for the tasks involved in your project, plus their flat fee as general contractor. Others will charge you *cost plus,* which is the cost of all materials and labor plus a percentage of the total budget, which is their fee. It's a toss-up as to which is better—just make sure you are keeping track of costs and understand what the actual cost is of each item.

DREW: Either way, the work should be itemized so you know how much you are paying for each job and all the materials. Contractors may give you allowances for certain items, such as lighting and flooring. (An *allowance* is money built in for certain items that you ofen choose yourself, such lighting fixtures, appliances, and flooring.) This should not be a problem if you can see the charges for those items, and the difference, if there is one, between the actual cost of the item and the allowance. Any savings should go back into your pocket at the end of the job.

JONATHAN: Don't forget that a written contract should lay out all details of the job, possibly including detailed drawings of the plans with elevations, the contractor's fees and mark-ups on materials, as well as how much change orders are. That's how much it costs when you change your mind about something after agreed-upon work starts, or if you add something on. Even I had a few add-ons when we were already well into the renovation of our Las Vegas house. Does a commercial grade waterslide count as an add-on? I guess it does.

DREW: Yeah, just a few add-ons! Change orders and add-ons can easily get out of control. Although I can say that Jonathan, in all his renovations, even ours, has never gone over budget for the original scope of work. Many budgets increase as homeowners insist on additional features. If you didn't price out a fully custom walk-in closet or a Swedish sauna in the master, don't expect that those items are going to magically fit into your original budget unless you remove other items to balance out the costs. The contract should specify how much change orders are and what delays (because of add-ons or other things) will cost. Communicate as soon as possible about any changes you want to make.

JONATHAN: Of course you want to touch base with the contractor when work is going on, and in-person is best. Just *don't* micromanage. If you did your homework to find a good contractor, trust him to do the job. Any time you do discuss something, always follow up by detailing in writing what you discussed. I love email because it provides a paperless "paper trail." So all communication, even after I talk with a client, is covered with a follow-up email.

DREW: Ultimately, you want to have a friendly and professional working relationship with all the pros on your project. All the effort you put into identifying the right people is worth it when that sledgehammer comes down on that fake wood paneling the morning of Day One.

JONATHAN: But if you run into serious trouble such as a breach of contract or badly done work, you can file a complaint with a licensing bureau (with licensed professionals), and the situation will be verified and inspected. Valid complaints can result in fines, suspensions, or loss of license. Otherwise, your only real recourse is to take the contractor to court, and that can be costly and often not worthwhile.

Who Does What

On the following pages is our cheat sheet of the basic building trades and what they do. There are actually many more specialized trades than those listed, but these are the ones you're most likely to run into on your job.

Make sure you understand licensing and credential rules in your state and community since every state has different licensing laws. For example, structural engineers need a license to work in all 50 states, but state licenses normally allow engineers to work only in the issuing state, which is why many engineers have licenses from more than one state. Other trades are less consistent, state-by-state, in licensing requirements. According to the most recent data, in Pennsylvania general contractors don't need a license, but in North Dakota contractors must have a license to work on any job costing $2,000 or more. However, in Texas only specialty contractors, including HVAC, fire sprinkler systems experts, plumbers, and well drilling/pump installation specialists need to be licensed. In New York, aside from asbestos abatement work, all construction work is regulated and licensed at the local or community level. Check the most recent requirements in your area for up-to-date licensing laws.

This is just a snapshot of how different states regulate the construction industry and its related fields. Confusing, we know. So, whether or not you live in a state that requires your general contractor to have a license, you must ask him or her what licenses are needed to perform which work on your job—and to make sure licensed professionals are hired when required. This is important because you may not get permits or pass inspections if work is not done by properly licensed pros.

The interesting thing is, just because someone has a license doesn't mean they are good at what they do. The government does not look into how experienced or how skilled they are, so a license is absolutely not a guarantee of excellence or even competence. A lot of people barely passed licensing and may have never handled your type of project. It's kind of like, just because Drew puts on a tool belt and a plaid shirt, doesn't mean he's going to be as good as Jonathan at renovating your bathroom. Okay, it's not an exact comparison, but it still happens to be true. (But if you ask Drew, he'll definitely claim to be better-looking in a tool belt.) So to recap, do check references, look at previous work, and get a feel for the person before hiring—use common sense.

Carpenters can create cabinetry and other casework and moldings for your specific needs, taste ... and budgets.

CARPENTER: Makes and installs cabinetry, creates and installs millwork (like crown and baseboard molding), frames walls, installs flooring, and makes furniture.

CARPET LAYER: Installs carpet on floors and stairs.

DRYWALLER: Handles insulation installation, drywall boarding, and mudding.

ELECTRICIAN: Handles anything "powered" like lighting, wiring, and panel work. Only hire an electrician who has a license.

GLAZIER (GLASS INSTALLER): Installs all types of glass such as new windowpanes, railings, and glass shower doors.

HVAC: Stands for heating, ventilation, and air conditioning. That pretty much says it … although these mechanical techs will also usually run and test your gas lines too.

LABORER: Assists tradesman with various jobs including painting, installing drywall, assembling various built-ins, millwork, and decking.

LANDSCAPER: Handles both heavy and small equipment to create gardenscapes and outdoor features.

MASON: Specializes in laying brick and stone. Creates retained walls, patios, fireplaces, and anything else having to do with stonework.

Stonework is an art—masons can create beautiful, natural features inside and out.

PAINTER: Specializes in painting and texturing and other special paint effects.

PLUMBER: Keeps your toilet working but also creates the entire plumbing system for a project, including where pipes go and how they connect. The only person who can install a radiant hot water in-floor heating system.

There is a lot of science behind a properly plumbed house.

WELDER: Welds any metals to create structure or features such as fences, stair railings, and fireplace screens.

Ironwork is another specialty that can bring unique style to a home.

The DIY-Possible List

We realize you may be talented and feel confident about your handyman (or handywoman) skills and are eager to do some work in your house. There are money-saving projects that even beginners can handle but that won't lead to disaster. Here's our list of projects homeowners can tackle on their own, including those of you who may feel slightly DIY-challenged.

> **PAINTING:** You can't make too many mistakes with painting unless you pick the wrong color. Success is all in the prep. Be sure to cover flooring with a sturdy canvas drop cloth. Canvas drop cloths are the most expensive, but they last a lifetime—that's why the pros use them. Try to forgo cheap plastic drop cloths; they are notoriously slippery, and that means dangerous. If you have to use plastic, tape all the edges down to minimize possible slipping.

> Make sure you remove all plate covers, grilles, and curtains so that you have an unobstructed canvas on which to paint. Painter's tape will become your best friend. Make sure everything is completely covered with it, from trim to hinges. *Do not* paint over hinges. It's one of Jonathan's pet peeves and it's possible that he'll throttle the next homeowner whom he sees do this! It looks terrible and it's very unprofessional. It can also prevent the hinges from working properly. To prevent the tape from bleeding paint, put a very small amount of paint on your brush and run it along the inside seam or the side that you are painting. This seals the edge and allows you to apply a thick roller coat without any mishaps.

> For best results, only use new, lint-free rollers. Previously used rollers don't cover as well, and unless you're a very experienced painter, you need all the help you can get.

LEAVE THESE JOBS TO THE PROS:

> HVAC
> Mudding and drywall
> Electrical
> Roofing
> Framing ... and anything structural

Painting can be a great DIY job,
but if you want a special effect,
a pro may be your best bet.

> **SOME DEMO WORK:** Just take safety precautions. Eye protection, gloves, and sturdy footwear are non-negotiable. Most accidents on a construction site happen as a result of something dumb like stepping on a nail or cutting yourself on something sharp. So slow it down, and play it safe. Never remove studs from a wall unless it has been confirmed by a pro that it isn't load bearing, or the entire house could come crashing down on you. Signs of a load-bearing wall are things like a double top plate (two 2x4s at the top of the wall), joists resting on the wall in the opposite direction, headers above doors or windows, and posts built up inside the wall.

> And don't wildly smash into walls, as they may house water pipes, electrical, or ducting. I'm sure the last thing you want is to cause a flood! Believe us, Jonathan has had floods on a couple of projects, and it is a nightmare. You can ruin your brand new cabinets and floors and short out electrical. One of the most common causes of a leak during construction is a screw piercing a water line during the drywall phase. So always ensure you know where you're screwing into the studs, have your water lines and electrical centered in the wall cavity, and inspect for any signs of a leak *before* closing up the walls. House floods are not good for your budget … or your self-esteem.

> Always carefully peel back the surface to inspect inside the wall cavity. If clear, then you can smash through to the other side. Also research to make sure there aren't any known environmental hazards in your area with your age of home. You can test for asbestos, lead, etc., if you fear there may be contaminated material in your project. The older the home, the more contaminants there can be, especially if the home was built in the 1970s or earlier. There can be asbestos in the plaster, popcorn ceilings, floor tile, and so on. Research construction practices of your area for known concerns, talk to local pros, and test before you smash.

> **REMOVING POPCORN CEILINGS:** This is one of the messiest jobs you can tackle around the house, and even though you'll have popcorn ceiling gunk all over your work clothes, and probably in your hair, this is a DIY job that can save you big time on labor costs. Make sure you remove all furniture from the space, and place a thick drop cloth down in the room where you're working. Also, wear old clothes and goggles because wet compound can bleach out clothing and sting the eyes. Dip a thick ceiling paint roller into warm water and roll it onto the ceiling. Let the water sit on the popcorn for a couple of minutes until it is thoroughly saturated with warm water. Then get scraping using a 4- or 6-inch putty knife. Be careful not to gouge the drywall or plaster, as you only want to scrape the excess texture off. There is a caveat: Any house more than 40 years old could have asbestos in the popcorn, so get it tested before you begin.

A coffered ceiling like this
obviously has to be created by
a master carpenter, if you want
a professional result.

Painting a piece of furniture or cabinetry work is definitely something a confident DIYer can tackle.

❯ STRIPPING, REFINISHING, AND PAINTING WOOD FURNITURE AND WOODWORK: We often use existing built-ins like cabinetry and shelves or vintage pieces of furniture in our renovations, and making them feel fresh and new again is a job even amateurs can enjoy and feel proud of. If Jonathan had a nickel for every time homeowners walked into a final design and didn't recognize one of their own pieces ... well, he'd have about $5. You can bring that wow factor back without having to buy all new. Even tired woodwork can be given new life with a new stain, re-stain, or coat of paint. It's funny because Drew will paint over any woodwork at the drop of the hat. However, some people refuse to ever paint over wood at any time. Well, our feeling is that there's a time and a place for everything: Just because an old feature in your home is made from wood doesn't mean you can't paint over it if you want a more contemporary feel. But if it's a neighborhood where buyers search out homes with original exposed wood, maybe think twice. It's laborious, but if you've got the time and patience, refreshing any item yourself can save you money and give you a new skill to brag about. And think about it this way: Painting out the old wood tones is not ruining the traditional woodwork feature—it's breathing fresh life into it!

Switching out bathroom faucets is easier than you may think.

> **REPLACING SOME FIXTURES:** Sometimes there's no sense in ripping everything out if you don't need to. If you're looking for ways to update while still keeping money in your pocket, perhaps consider keeping the original sinks and countertops in the kitchen or bathrooms if they are not in bad shape and changing the faucets. It's a straightforward job to simply replace and update the faucets or even showerheads. Just make sure the water is turned off, disconnect the lines marking which line is hot and which is cold, measure the holes, ensure the new fixture will fit, use Teflon tape or similar product on the connection, and follow the manufacturer's instructions to complete the installation. Sounds like a lot of steps, but it's actually quite easy … and now you don't have to stare at that ugly brass faucet any longer.

> INSTALLING OFF-THE-SHELF CLOSET ORGANIZATION SYSTEMS: A standard closet can hold more and stay neater with a closet system. Most big box home centers offer shelving and other organizational systems at a fraction of the cost of custom closet systems, and they are designed to be DIY projects. Make sure you still take very accurate measurements of your closet and figure out a design that will maximize the use of space. There shouldn't be any awkward corners or difficult, tight spaces to access. When you figure out the best layout, find the prefab shelving that will fit best. Every big box store has more than one option, and you won't need anything special to assemble. Usually a hammer, screwdriver, and some patience are all you need to get the job done. Well, of course it helps when you have a contractor brother too! Ensure that the organizational system is secured properly to a solid stud where required. Grab some extra material to fill in any gaps (usually made by the system manufacturer), and even consider installing a back panel and crown molding, which will make it feel more like a custom closet. At the end of the day, an organized closet will allow for much more storage … and a lot less gray hair trying to find what you're looking for when you are in rush to get out the door.

OPPOSITE: Closet systems available at home stores make for a great weekend project.

ABOVE: Installing engineered hardwood or laminate floating floors is a project that an intermediate DIYer can accomplish.

〉 INSTALLING LAMINATE FLOORING: It's a breeze to do and there are tons of great how-to videos online that'll show you all the tips and tricks. Here are the main points we want you to consider about this job: Pick a good-quality, single-board laminate. The dated 8-inch-wide laminate doesn't add any value, whereas a 10- or 12-inch board is more modern and looks more like real engineered hardwood. Make sure you don't line up the seams from row to row within 6 inches of each other. You want it to look totally random. Get the right type of transition strip because you don't want to see the edge of the laminate. Jonathan's preferred method of installation is

to glue down the material with a product like DriTac, as it eliminates the hollow sound that floating floors have, and provides a moisture barrier and sound dampening too. You don't need any more than a rubber mallet, notched trowel, painter's tape, table saw, and miter saw to complete the install. Leave yourself about one inch of space all the way around so that the floor can expand and contract from season to season. This gap will be covered by the baseboard or shoe mold if you're not installing new base. If done correctly and with the right laminate product, nobody will be able to differentiate the flooring from engineered hardwood.

❯ BASIC TILING: If you're up for it, installing a kitchen backsplash is a job any homeowner can handle. We recommend first watching tutorials on YouTube and taking one of the tiling classes that are offered regularly at large home building centers. Make sure you prep the wall properly (which may involve replacing broken drywall). We recommend either Greenboard or a backer board meant for tile, as it is better in an environment that can get splashed with water. Depending on the pattern and style of tile you choose, just ensure your lines are all straight. If it's a mosaic tile, stop from time to time and step back to ensure you aren't creating any unintentional patterns. This is a job that can get messy so cover your counters well and don't put on too much adhesive. For a backsplash you can use mastic that is applied with a V-notch trowel. Do a few feet at a time as you go. Do not leave excess mastic sitting on the wall too long, as it will start to cure and become less effective. Depending on the type of tile you purchase, cutting can be different. In most cases you want a good wet saw with a new blade. The more you do, the faster you'll get. You could probably complete the average kitchen within a few hours. Easy weekend job. You'll be fine.

Mosaic tiles, which come in sheets, are among the easiest for DIYers since there is often less cutting involved.

TO LIVE OR NOT TO LIVE …
In Your Reno

In the best of all possible worlds, you would not live in your renovation. It's hard enough to live through a renovation from a distance. In a basement or one-room living situation, you might have use of only a microwave or you may only have a regular closet instead of a walk-in. The added stress of having to make coffee in a powder room and dinner in the unfinished basement week after week … after week is enough to drive many people over the edge. We plead with homeowners not to stay in a house that is undergoing a major renovation. They swear they can tough it out and won't get in the way. But often after the first workday they complain about workers who show up at 7 a.m. and start making noise.

Yes, some families do choose to live in the basement of their house, or decamp to the upstairs bedrooms, but it's not an ideal situation. There is a lot of dust, dirt, and construction chaos during a renovation. That's why some of our clients choose to stay with relatives or friends during the work period, or in their current house, extending the closing as long as possible if they have sold that house. Getting a modest rental home or apartment while it is happening is also an option—another costly part of renovation that should be calculated into your overall budget.

It comes down to budget, and many people can't afford to put themselves up in a hotel or rent a house while their new house in under construction. We worked with a family of five who were determined to stay in the basement of their house mainly because of finances. Four of them slept in a king-sized bed and one of the children camped out in a sleeping bag on the floor. The sleeping arrangements weren't the biggest headache they faced—the mom was into clothes and did not want to downsize her wardrobe for the duration of the project … so she jammed every outfit and pair of shoes into the basement space too. It was tough on them to crowd everything and everyone in one area, but they muddled through. Tempers often ran hot and no one was ever in a great mood. This is a prime example of where it makes sense to call in your favor card with the in-laws or a friend. Besides, who wouldn't want you to stay with them for a few weeks?

You will not only be space-challenged if you live in your reno project. With construction going on, you will be sharing the heating and cooling systems with the workers and they will share their dust with you through those same vents. In that case, make sure you tape off registers in the construction zone so they are not sucking in dust and then transferring it into the area you've encamped to. You can buy thick plastic panels and special plastic zippers that attach to create seals between doorways that keep dust out of non-construction areas. But you can still go in and out of the room easily. Surface Shields and Tarp Zipper are two of the manufacturers of these zippers, which are available in home stores.

Anyone with asthma or respiratory issues should seriously consider living elsewhere while construction is going on. Otherwise, you'll wake up with a sore throat and a cough because the atmosphere is less than perfect. People with very young children, babies, or small pets like cats and birds are taking a huge risk by staying in a construction zone for the same reasons—these small beings are more vulnerable to poor air conditions than healthy adults.

If you are a light sleeper, it's not a good idea to live in the construction site either. We have very tight deadlines on TV, and one client told us we could not start until 10 a.m., and we had to stop at 7 p.m. Normally, we work from 9 a.m. to 9 p.m. to make show deadlines. But these clients wanted to sleep, and get their kids ready for school, without any workers around. For most contractors, a 9 a.m. start time is late—you might be faced with workers who show up at 7 a.m. and knock off at 4 p.m. If you don't want workers around while you're having coffee and getting dressed for work, a hotel might be a good bet.

Out with the old means in with the new! Let's move on to the exciting and creative part of renovation—deciding what to put into your new space after all the old stuff comes out.

"REALTY" CHECK: INVISIBLE ISSUES

Don't get mad at the contractor if something surprising is revealed in your renovation! No one has X-ray vision, and your contractor will undoubtedly uncover problems that he (or an inspector) did not see when the home was initially assessed. Some problems just don't show up until the walls come down and the sinks come out. This happens to us all the time. That's why any contractor's budget or estimate should include a contingency fund of at least 10 percent for unknown eventualities. If there are a lot of known issues in your community, bump that contingency up. We've had them as high as 25 percent of the total budget before. Expect surprises!

SPACE RACE

GET THE ROOM (AND THE ROOMS) YOU WANT

Renovation is hard work. It's often frustrating and unpredictable, but the payoff can be absolutely amazing. When we were redoing our Las Vegas home, we contended with theft (a real problem on construction sites), unexpected plumbing and electrical issues, work delays, and broken or damaged materials—everything that happens on other people's renovations happened on ours. But like we said, the end result is amazing. When you tackle a whole house reno, or even just a makeover of a room or two, you're taking something tired and breathing new life into it so you, as well as the generation after you, can enjoy it.

By using an existing house to create your dream space, you're also being kind to the planet. It's like repurposing on a grander scale … with a whole house. If you use sustainable materials as well, then you're maximizing the positive impact your property will have on the environment (we talk about just that in Chapter 6, Material Matters, page 209).

Rehabs fit perfectly into the green mantra, "Renew, reuse, recycle." According to a study, *The Greenest*

A few modifications transform a plain master bedroom into a chic master suite.

Building by the National Trust for Historic Preservation, in almost every instance, remodeling an old building is greener than building a new one. That's because a new building operating at 30 percent greater efficiency than an existing building can take between 10 and 80 years to overcome the environmental impact created by construction. So let's fix up an old house and make it more efficient, and you can experience new function and style in a vintage house.

A tidy, monochromatic bathroom with modern fixtures makes a small space seem larger.

BELOW: A tray ceiling, new window treatments, and better lighting make this boy's room a cool hangout.

OPPOSITE: Carving out a pantry in a kitchen can double your food storage space. A sliding door is a fashionable space saver.

AFTER

BROTHER VS. BROTHER:

Dream Big!

DREW: When I ask clients to tell me what they want in a home, I hear a lot of the same thing: "I want a dream house with a beautiful, modern kitchen, a spa-like bathroom, and four spacious bedrooms." Who *doesn't* want those things? The client often has a hard time getting more specific than that because dreaming up the perfect house is overwhelming. In order to steer them to houses that fit their buying and reno budget, I usually start with some fun. We create a wish list. I ask the client to spend some time writing down everything they can think of that they might like to have, no matter how wild. Even a golden toilet ... whatever is dreamy to them.

JONATHAN: From there we give them their first reality check and ask them to divide that list into must-haves and nice-to-haves, something we talked about in Chapter 1, although this list really drills down much more deeply into everything they've ever thought of as being nice to have. Sometimes we have to go through the list several times before the clients get to a realistic, doable point that matches their budget.

DREW: If they are having trouble getting real, I'm more than happy to take buyers to look at a dream home that is out of their financial league and see what they respond to. It's often easier for people to see elements of a house they didn't know about or realize would be useful. On these dream house tours, I observe and make note of what really impresses them. We add those things to the list and take off other things that, once they see, they realize are not as important as they thought. For instance, one family with kids and

pets were convinced they wanted hardwood floors throughout their house. We showed them a house with hardwood floors, which had been inhabited by a family with ... kids and pets. They could very clearly see the damage that was done to the floors in terms of scratches, dings, and even some deep grooves. Most of the flooring needed refinishing, and some needed replacement—and this was not an old house. Seeing how vulnerable wood floors are to family life really made them think twice about what they wanted. Ultimately, they agreed with Jonathan that vinyl plank flooring that looks identical to engineered hardwood would be a better choice for their lifestyle. To mimic this experience look for model homes that are open to the public. These homes normally have all the upgrades so you can see many features and decide whether they are important to you or not.

JONATHAN: On *Property Brothers* I always dread the moment when Drew spills the beans about the price of the "bells-and-whistles" houses. It's a harsh form of tough love, showing them a completely renovated, high-end turnkey house with everything on their extensive wish list that may not fit into their budget. The shock usually takes a few minutes to wear off, then once they realize the reason Drew did this, they agree that a fixer-upper is the way to go. The clients then have to make a decision about what they want to do with their renovation money. What is more important? The man cave or the mudroom? The second living area or the fireplace? Sometimes they have to give up on their original idea of the perfect master bathroom with a separate tub and shower because it just won't fit the space of the house they have purchased. We have to remind them that there isn't just one right way to make over a space. So they can still get an incredible master bath with all the style and function they desire but may have to accept some slightly compromised features. On a positive note, it will suit their finances. It's in no way a miracle when I swoop in and save the day by designing an alternate bathroom that works for the client (well, maybe it is my super power), rather it's simply a fun case of problem solving where there is always a solution that will work. And not only that, the fixer is customized exactly to their tastes. Even the priciest move-in-ready dream home can't boast that.

DREW: Actually, *I* save the day when I negotiate a great price for the fixer-upper and save them money so they can get all their must-haves into the space. We both definitely emphasize space concerns, because everyone always wants more. I look for beat-up houses with the square footage to accommodate a client's needs, because working within an existing footprint is more cost effective than building up or out from scratch.

JONATHAN: Sure, you may get the house at a good price, but who makes the reno budget work? That would be me. In fact, when Drew takes them through the dream home the clients get even more ideas on their wish list. Yet, my budget remains the same. And in some circumstances the clients pay more for the original purchase, giving me less reno money to work with, but I'm still expected to pull off everything on the list. Sooo Drew, what day are you saving again? Ha-ha. As we walk through properties, Drew and I both point out to clients how the spaces in a house can be enlarged, enhanced, and improved. We really want to open homeowners' eyes to possibilities. For instance, kitchens with cabinets that don't go up to the ceiling are a waste of space. Bringing the cabinets right up to the ceiling adds up to 30 percent more storage, and it's not a budget buster. That said, storage is the one place where people often end up making concessions in exchange for bling in the finishes—and then regret it later. People tend to assign more importance to a pretty kitchen or nice bathrooms, and are often willing to forgo function and storage until they move in. As they unpack, they say, "Oh shoot, I don't have enough room." If I was given free rein by a client to design a space, it would have tons of storage.

DREW: We also caution homeowners to adjust their expectations about the renovation of an older home. Nothing is going to be completely perfect, level, flush, and plumb when building new over old. You can visually minimize imperfections, but your house is never going to be completely free of "flaws," so be realistic and embrace the small quirks as character.

As long as you do a quality renovation, then small quirks are not a problem in terms of resale. Idiosyncratic houses—homes with unique floor plans, ones that are made from unusual materials, or even off-the-grid homes, are another story because there aren't a lot of available comps. These houses can be tougher to sell and trickier to finance because lenders are queasy about giving these oddballs a mortgage for the amount that you think it should be worth.

JUST BECAUSE IT'S OLD
Doesn't Mean It's Good

Houses ripe for renovation and restoration often have original features, and many people believe that if something is original to the house it should be preserved. It might be sacrilege to some preservationists to say this, but that's not always true. Not every older home is an important example of its architectural style or in a safe/healthy state to occupy. Here's another news flash: Not every original feature is intrinsically in good shape, or was high quality to begin with. Understand the difference between a feature that's worth keeping and those that can be replaced without remorse. Original hardwood floors in older homes are not always salvageable. They may be badly stained, water damaged and warped, rotted, or sanded so often they are thin and worn. Or sometimes the original boards are far too costly to match up and patch. So don't feel bad about getting rid of them. Some of the wood could even be recycled and used to make other things.

You can pretty much repurpose any material/fixture in a home. You'd be amazed at what people will buy or simply take off your hands if free. Unfortunately, we don't have time in the shows to showcase what we do with houses' old parts, but most often we list reusable materials online to either sell them (which can help with renovation costs), or give them away to an organization like Habitat for Humanity. Sometimes if Habitat can't take something, we'll place material and fixtures on the front lawn with a FREE sign. I'm sure you won't be surprised to learn that fellow renovators scoop up those items for use in their own projects. At the end of the day, it's all about trying to reduce how much winds up in a landfill.

When we renovated a 110-year-old house, we removed the original studs on one floor to open up the space. They were made in the early 1900s, when the wood measured exactly two by four inches. Jonathan cleaned up the studs by pulling the nails out of them. Since he was having trouble finding the right sized table for the long, narrow dining area, he asked a friend of ours who's an amazing woodworker to make a table from the studs. He laminated the studs together, sanded the resulting slab, and then cut it to size. It was mounted on a base and became a gorgeous, custom table for the family. A piece of history that came directly from the house is now the centerpiece of the homeowners' kitchen and dining area.

We've taken the stone from an old kitchen island and had it re-cut to make tabletops. We reupholster chairs, repaint lamps and furniture, and repurpose old kitchen cabinets as storage in a garage or workshop. The only time we toss something is when it's

Floor Plan Fixes

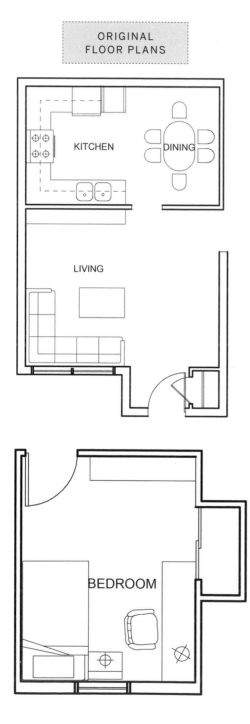

KITCHEN

DINING

LIVING

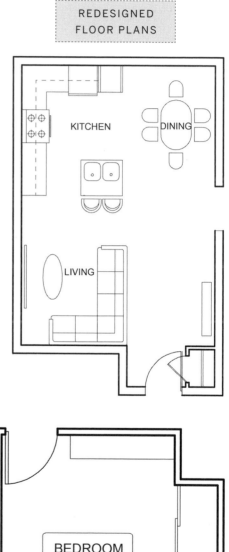

KITCHEN

DINING

LIVING

BEDROOM

BEDROOM

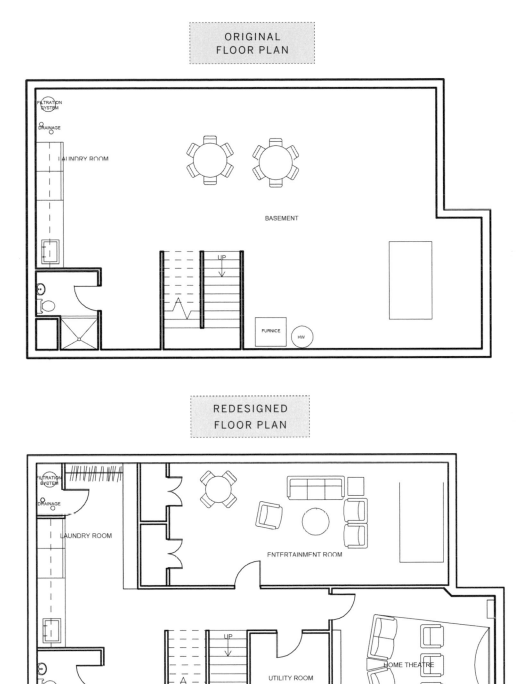

We used the original hardwood studs from this home to create a dining table.

cheaply made, or falls apart during demo. Sometimes, especially in older homes, kitchen cabinets are so well constructed, and built in place, that you cannot remove them without destroying the boxes. Every situation is different, but we can guarantee you that a lot more can be repurposed than you think.

But don't just keep something because it's old. It needs to serve some purpose, either functionally or aesthetically. If the built-in cabinets or shelving no longer serves a modern purpose in a family space, replace them with those that are more functional. Old fireplace surrounds are not sacrosanct—they can be ugly, impractical (no mantel), or damaged. Replacing them with a more modern alternative can give a living space an almost instant facelift. Even moldings around windows, doors, and baseboards can be removed if they aren't of good quality. Your guests should never walk in after a renovation and question what materials and features are new.

What if the original feature is in good shape, but you just don't like it? Well, that's a decision you have to make. We recommend talking to a local real estate expert to see if these specific features will devalue the house if taken out. If the answer is no, remove the feature carefully because you may be able to donate it to Habitat's ReStore or a similar organization, or sell it to someone who does like it and can use in their own home renovation project. If the answer is yes and removing the feature would decrease the home's value, you have two choices: You can remove and store it carefully so it can be reinstalled if the next homeowner appreciates it more than you do. Or try to improve the space around it and do your best to make it blend better.

The big debate we always have with each other is about the original woodwork: *To Paint or Not to Paint*. Drew is happy to paint everything, all the time, in order to modernize. Jonathan agrees crisp white paint on trim and molding can refresh a room, but what if "modern" isn't what you're going for? Or what if you love the look of natural wood? Then, maybe you should keep the original wood and re-stain it.

There are some features intrinsic to certain houses that are worth maintaining and even restoring. A beautiful old two-story home we worked on had a very nice original staircase and a small stained glass window in the stairwell. Both of these charming features gave the house character and spoke to its history so we kept them, fixing and refinishing anything that needed to be repaired. A 1970s house we worked on had high-quality, custom-made built-in cabinetry along one wall of its large family room. We were able to keep that feature, which incorporated the fireplace and a television cabinet. With some paint and minor alternations to retrofit the cabinet to accommodate a flat screen TV, the built-in had character and was no longer outdated.

If you buy a truly historic home, and you're unsure about which features are important and which ones can go, consult a local historical society or an architect who specializes in

Painting woodwork and trim modernizes a space.

Stained wood trim can be very traditional or rustic, depending on your taste.

vintage houses. Keep in mind that many heritage homes require historical society approval on all work you do, inside and out. Historic commissions can be quite strict with what methods and materials you use. They often demand that you use the exact materials that were used when the home was built, and some of these materials, like certain types of wood (mahogany, walnut) can be much more expensive than modern alternatives. That means these restorations can be double or triple the costs of those of an average renovation. When buying a heritage home, know what adventure you're about to embark on.

This magnificent stained glass window is original to the house, so we kept it and incorporated it into the new design. It was in great shape and speaks to the home's 1920s era and style. It also adds a nice pop of color to a fairly monochromatic color scheme.

The built-in along the 1970s family room wall presented more opportunities than obstacles for the home's redo, so we kept it. We opted to tweak it a bit (and paint it, of course) so that it looked more contemporary. A retrofit of a closed cabinet created a niche for the homeowners' flat screen television.

FIVE MYTHS ABOUT
Remaking Great Spaces

We want to bust some myths about renovation and clear up some common misconceptions.

MYTH #1:
A HOUSE WITH MASS APPEAL IS BORING AND COOKIE CUTTER.

People often translate our advice to keep future buyers in mind when renovating into making sure every finish in the house is neutral, beige, and bland. This is not at all what we mean. Nobody says they dream of one day owning a boring house with no color! Granted, you probably don't want to paint neon pink polka dots on the living room wall (unless you are willing to paint over them when you put your house on the market). However, there are many ways to be bold and unique without going overboard. We advocate approaching a renovation with a classic sensibility that's also fresh and modern. That translates to clean lines, interesting textural materials, and pops of colors supplied by accessories and textiles that are easier to replace or update than more permanent materials, such as flooring and wall coverings.

MYTH #2:
ALL RENOVATIONS INCREASE THE VALUE OF THE HOUSE.

This common line of thinking simply isn't true (see our list of Reno No-Nos on page 206). There are many "improvements" that are of no interest to future buyers; so after spending all that time and money, you're unlikely to get it back when you're ready to sell. Smart renovation is all about how you approach your wants

and needs. The secret room off the master bedroom that hides your vintage *Star Wars* paraphernalia in a custom Plexiglas cabinet shaped like the Death Star probably won't speak to everyone (although it would be cool). Instead, store your collections in a devoted room, but keep the room itself flexible enough to be easily used for something else later, such as a home office—a must-have for a lot of people. You can personalize these spaces through décor (we'll show you how in Chapter 7, Feathering Your Nest, page 237) without making the bones of the rooms and the fixtures so particular that they date quickly or are just too quirky for an easy resale. Make the most of your space, make it work for you, and get your must-haves, but do it in a smart way, with both resale and long-term value in mind.

MYTH #3:
IF YOU CAN DREAM IT, YOU CAN DO IT!

In theory, that might be right. But practically speaking, the International Building Code (and some communities) may not look too kindly on all of your construction and design ideas. So before you install a grid of 4 x 4-inch windows in a bedroom, your contractor will have to check with the city to see if you can get permission. This would require a development permit, in addition to the building permit. Some simple building permits can take as little as a day, as in on-the-spot, right-at-the-counter permission, whereas other permits can take weeks. Development permits are even worse, or you might be turned down completely if your plans do not fit with prevailing construction rules and regulations in the area. As for your grid system window, International Building Code requires that at least one window in every bedroom be large enough to permit the occupants to escape in the event of a fire. There is also a restriction as to how many "fire penetrations" (windows) you can have in the side of a building if you face another building, so you may not be allowed to add any additional windows at all. Likewise, community rules might prohibit you from building a new structure, such as an addition, over a certain height or width. Save yourself headaches (and possible work shutdowns and fines), and know the rules of your municipality. A professional who renovates in your area should know the local construction restrictions and limitations. An architect will definitely be aware of what you can and can't do. That said, there are plenty of creative things to do inside a house, as long as they are safe and legal, from moving and removing walls to reconfiguring bedrooms to creating interesting staircases, reading niches, and play spaces. But remember, the more you do, the more it costs!

MYTH #4:
YOU CAN'T OVERDO QUALITY.

There's no sense in building everything within the house to withstand a bomb blast. It's just not feasible, and your budget would have to be three times bigger than it probably is. There are a variety of materials available if, depending on the project and what the neighborhood demands, you want to go more or less expensive. We use the best-quality materials we can afford with the budgets on each specific project. However, we always keep that future resale value in mind. Don't over-renovate for the neighborhood with changes that are too high-end, trendy, or obscure, because these kinds of renovations actually devalue the property. Trying to sell a $500,000 house in a $200,000 neighborhood? Good luck. If no one else in the neighborhood has designer 12-inch-wide hand-scraped hardwood flooring, stone counters, and professional-grade kitchen appliances, people who are looking to buy in that neighborhood won't expect to see them in a house and won't be willing to pay a premium for them. Understand the market you're in so your renovations can be in keeping with what the neighbors are doing and what the market can bear. You can always do something that makes your house stand out ahead of the competition, just don't go overboard. When buying materials, use the philosophy "best in class or category." In other words, if it's a first-time-buyer neighborhood, prefab cabinets are absolutely okay, as no first-time buyer can afford a fully custom kitchen. As long as you finish off the cabinets the best way possible with trim and crown, it'll look like an amazing kitchen that the buyer would be thrilled to have as their own.

MYTH #5:
YOU HAVE TO PROVIDE DETAILED DRAWINGS FOR CONTRACTORS AND ARCHITECTS.

There's no need to use custom 3D renderings like the ones offered up on our shows, which are quite expensive to create. We use them on the show because television is obviously a visual medium, and anything that helps viewers get excited about a project is a bonus. In real life, a pencil (with a big eraser) and some graph paper are all the tools you need to imagine and re-imagine your new space. And it's enough information for an architect or engineer to create the drawings needed for permits, approvals, and the trades to get their work done. "Off the rack" design software programs are a more high-tech, but still affordable, option for renovation and space planning. Oh, and please don't say to your contractor … "Well the Property Brothers do a 3D design, why don't you?" They hate that. The easiest thing to do is to create an inspiration folder or a mood board with photos of rooms, features, textures, and colors that you like. We've even created an app that can help you do this and is essentially an easy way to gather your thoughts on a project to keep yourself organized.

Ultimately, it doesn't matter what method you use to visualize and communicate information on your renovation. A graphic representation of your ideas is simply a visual way of expressing what you want to do with a space. As long as the format you use clearly indicates the walls you want to move and the features you want in the house, a professional can translate it into usable plans. The finished product is the only thing that really counts— and whatever method makes you happy. Some of our tech-savvy clients love to spend hours creating their own detailed plans. That's amazing but totally unnecessary, as we still have to redo them in our CAD software. But again, if it makes you happy … get your rocks off.

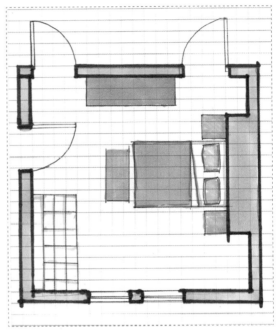

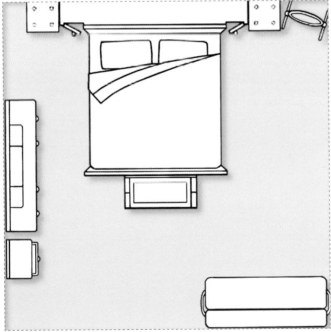

Side-by-side images of one
of the Property Brothers' 3D
renderings, a simple room layout
produced with basic software,
and a hand-drawn layout on
graph paper

This renovated kitchen includes a space-saving island because a wall that enclosed the original kitchen was removed. Now the kitchen connects to the adjacent living space, and the island serves as an impromptu eating area.

Smart Reno Moves

Here is our checklist of the renovations that give you the best return on investment, but also give you the most enjoyment and functionality in your home.

☐ **OPEN FLOOR PLAN:** Boxed in, tiny kitchens cut off the social function of a house. In the past, you wanted to shut out the noises of the kitchen—but now it's all part of the enjoyment of family and friends. The majority of older, un-renovated homes in North America are closed off and compartmentalized. The only way to bring a feeling of spaciousness to those homes and make them feel bigger is to open them up.

☐ **STORAGE:** No matter how we try to downsize, we've still got stuff. And home life is more pleasant if there's a place to put it. Adding storage in the basement, mudroom, bedrooms, and attic (or all of the above!) is a big plus for future buyers too. Look for creative storage solutions too, because you can never have too much. For instance, elevated shelving for bicycles and other gear in a garage helps keep lower areas clear. In one house we built hidden storage drawers right inside the first three steps of the stairway to the second floor. It was a great place to keep shoes and boots, dog leashes, gloves, and so on. Likewise, we love putting in toe-kick drawers on the bottom of lower kitchen cabinets; they are the perfect place to store large flat items like serving trays and baking

sheets. To one kitchen cabinet toe kick, we added a drawer for the family dog's dishes. Banquets and window seats can be built with hinged tops for loads of hidden storage. There is generally enough room on the inside of the pantry door to install storage racks and hooks. Sometimes Jonathan will screw a magnetic plate to the underside of a pantry shelf, which will hold numerous Mason jars (with metal lids) that can store all sorts of things.

☐ **HOT AND COOL STUFF:** Up-to-date, energy-efficient heating and cooling systems go a long way to making life more comfortable—and your monthly utility bills more affordable. These are big-ticket items that add a lot of value.

☐ **HIGH CEILINGS:** If there is plenty of space up in your attic, depending on the roof structure, it can be pretty easy to vault the ceiling, giving you an additional five to ten feet in the room. High ceilings make a huge difference.

☐ **MASTER BATH:** A bath attached to the master bedroom in a house is a pleasant surprise, even for homebuyers who don't put it on their wish list. Sometimes an adjoining room can be converted to create a master bath and even a bigger walk-in closet.

☐ **DURABLE SURFACES:** We love materials like quartz and NeoLith for durability and no maintenance, but other products add beauty and value too, like marble and granite—they just need more maintenance. Try to avoid materials that scratch too easily because you'll shed a single tear when you scuff them up within the first week. Solid surface flooring takes many forms as well. Take your pick of tile, hardwood, single board laminate, or vinyl plank; most people prefer an easy-to-care-for floor to high-maintenance, allergen-collecting wall-to-wall carpet.

☐ **CUSTOM CLOSETS:** A great closet system, with shelving and multiple height rods, is a bonus for you and future buyers. This is especially true if you have no room in a master bedroom for a walk-in closet. A properly organized closet exploits existing space to its best advantage and many systems can be installed for only a few hundred dollars.

☐ **FINISHED BASEMENT:** Real estate pros argue about this one, but we think anytime you can add finished storage or living space to a house it's worth it. It's also one of the least-intrusive but big-impact changes you can make to a home. Work can go on downstairs while you're living upstairs without too much stress and strain on the family. Just don't cut corners as basements need to be renovated properly or you'll have moisture problems. And really, really think about the best use of the space. A little extra work like putting in another bathroom may separate your place from other houses when you decide to sell.

☐ **NATURAL LIGHT:** We've yet to meet a buyer who tells us they want a dark house. There's probably one somewhere, hard at work looking for a good deal on a deep cave, but that person has never been a client of ours. Adding or enlarging windows is generally a safe bet if your home is noticeably dark. In addition to updating your home's look and enhancing curb appeal, installing new windows can help save on heating and cooling costs. Just be very careful to run the numbers because this is the one upgrade that can easily get out of control.

☐ **FUNCTIONAL, ATTRACTIVE EXTERIOR DOORS:** Updating an old manual garage door with new, automatic garage doors adds both curb appeal and functionality to the exterior of your house. New front and back doors do the same. A new front door can really brighten up a house and give it a whole new look without a lot of expense or work. Also consider swapping the back sliding door for beautiful French doors that open to your back deck.

Reno No-Nos

Of course, you want to emotionally connect with your home, but you can't allow emotions to steer the direction of your renovation. Just as there are features you want in a house, and that also increase the value of the space, there are changes you should not make to a house. These are features that can bite you back when it's time to sell and that may even start to annoy you after a while. We don't want you to make these mistakes. *So …*

1. DON'T TURN A SMALL THIRD BEDROOM INTO A WALK-IN CLOSET. In family-friendly neighborhoods, a house with three small bedrooms is still more valuable than a house with two bedrooms and a big closet. If you do commandeer a bedroom for storage, don't do anything that destroys the structural integrity of the room's "separateness." In other words, don't annex it to another bedroom, or close off a door that opens to a hallway.

2. DON'T GET RID OF THE ONLY BATHTUB. If you ever hope to sell your house to a family with kids, a house without a tub is going to be a turnoff. You don't have to have a bathtub in the master, unless the house is in a retirement community, but do keep a tub in the shared or family bathroom.

3. DON'T SPEND A FORTUNE BUILDING IN A CUSTOM HOME THEATER. Flat screen televisions will only continue to improve in terms of sound and picture quality. The components needed to create a feeling of being surrounded by sound will get smaller and less intrusive. The problem is that buyers say they love the idea of a movie room, but they're not willing to pay for it. In addition, technology is changing so fast that all this gear you spent a fortune on easily becomes dated … even if you sell in five years. Consider having some cool technology in a flexible space, like a family room that offers a variety of use. Wireless surround sound systems give you great sound without having to tear open walls; recessed lighting on dimmers in basements where ceilings are typically low and rooms dark gives you options for brightness in a room for watching movies. If you want both a fireplace in the family room and a TV and the only place to put the TV is over the fireplace, which can be too high for comfortable viewing, consider getting a high tech TV wall mount system that not only lets you tilt the screen to any angle, but also lets you pull the TV away from the wall and lower it to a more natural and comfortable height.

4. DON'T CONVERT A GARAGE INTO A FAMILY ROOM. Buyers expect to see a garage in communities that commonly feature them. So if your house is the odd man out, many buyers won't even look at it. If you need extra space for family gatherings, consider finishing the basement, or enclose a three-season porch and make it into a real room. Just don't permanently eliminate the garage; make sure it can easily be converted back if necessary.

5. DON'T PUT IN A POOL. In most cases a swimming pool does not add enough value to a house to offset the cost of putting it in. Not even close. In fact, many buyers consider them a maintenance hassle, and those with small children are often afraid of the safety risks associated with backyard pools. The only place a pool makes sense is in very warm climates where people spend time outside all year long. For instance, in Southern U.S. states and certain areas of California, a pool is an asset to you and future buyers. But still keep in mind you won't get *all* your money back for putting it in, even in these climates, mainly because of on-going maintenance and energy costs. So if you put one in you'd better use it a lot because from a financial standpoint it's still a no-no.

---

6. DON'T BUILD HIGHLY SPECIFIC ROOMS THAT CAN'T BE EASILY CHANGED. A bowling alley, indoor hot tub, indoor basketball court, wine cellar, and cigar room may have extremely limited appeal. Unless the market you're in can sustain these kinds of luxury add-ons, they just are not worth the money. Get a simple wine cooler and smoke your stogies outside!

"REALTY" CHECK: LAY THE GROUNDWORK

Go back to the nice-to-have list you made in Chapter 1 (page 48), and review it with your contractor to determine the groundwork necessary to make way for future projects. If you're planning on structural work, and you probably are, it makes economic sense to do as much of it up front as possible and prepare spaces for future improvements. For example, consider running the wiring for a surround sound system. In one home I worked on, I knew where the surround system would go when it was finally installed, so I installed the wiring, which is really nominal in terms of cost, and brought it through the walls, where I covered the openings with electrical plates. When the time comes to install the system, the plates can be removed and the openings are all set to accept the speakers. Run gas or plumbing to an area where you may add a feature later such as a bathroom, a new laundry room, a wet bar, or a kitchenette. The work can be done much more easily and cheaply when finances allow.

MATERIAL MATTERS

FIXTURES AND FINISHES

So many people dream of an indoor-outdoor flow in their homes, or a space with modern conveniences and technologies (even if their dream digs is a historic house). We wanted to bring the outdoors in when we renovated our Las Vegas house, which was built in 2008. Three standard windows and a hollow-core back door lined the back wall of the living area. These elements didn't exactly create the flow between the house and the soon-to-be backyard oasis and pool that we wanted. By installing a 10 x 22-foot collapsible windowed wall, which looks amazing, the house became instantly more sociable. We just open the accordion wall, and the living room and pool area become one enormous entertaining space.

It wasn't until the early 2000s that residential folding glass walls like the one we used were widely available to consumers. Today, such glass accordion walls can be placed virtually anywhere in a home. Depending on the manufacturer, many glass walls and folding doors are certified for use in hurricane areas.

Folding glass walls are just one of the amazing products available to homeowners today. By the time you finish reading this chapter, dozens of innovative new home improvement products and materials will either be in production or on their way to your nearest home store. From refrigerators that dispense sparkling water to custom tiles *you* design online for an off-the-rack price, home innovations continue to be more exciting in terms of originality, usefulness, and relevance to our at-home lives.

We can't talk about every new product on the market here; there's not enough space in the book, and we'd date ourselves even before we were done. Instead, we point out specific strides in the home marketplace that make attaining your must-haves more efficient and affordable. The main take-away of this chapter is to keep an open mind and open eyes. Don't settle for the same old thing! Be on the lookout for more and better products that make your life easier, while maintaining a high aesthetic standard. You can find inspiration everywhere you look.

BROTHER VS. BROTHER:

Rethink Manmade

JONATHAN: We want to bust the stigma surrounding manmade products, many of which are high-end in appearance and construction but still very affordable and eco-friendly. Case in point, laminate floors. The newest, single-board laminate flooring is durable, beautiful, and virtually indistinguishable from engineered hardwood. Dogs and children can destroy hardwood floors in as little as a year, so it's important to have something that'll stand up to the wear and tear of everyday family life. If you want to go a step further, a vinyl plank floor is nearly impervious to the abuse kids and pets dish out and will still look like new, year after year. Not only is it highly water resistant and

can even handle it if you drop a knife on it, but you can get right down on your hands and knees and touch it, and you can't tell that it isn't engineered hardwood. Ask Drew ... I fooled him.

DREW: I was just humoring Jonathan; I knew it wasn't the real thing. But whatever makes him happy. That vinyl plank was really high quality, which is why non-professionals (and even some professionals) often can't tell the difference. As in all home improvement products, there is a variety of grades (or quality) in manmade flooring. Always go for the best quality you can afford, no matter what material you use. This is a smart move for your life in the house, and in terms of resale. Look at warranties, noting the length as well as the conditions under which the product is guaranteed. If you want to put laminate in your kitchen and bath, make sure the product warranties use of the product in rooms with water exposure. Some laminate products are

completely waterproof, others just water-resistant. The longer the warranty and the broader the uses for the flooring, the better quality it is. For instance, a 25-year residential warranty that guarantees the joints between pieces will remain closed and the color won't fade or change from exposure to the sun is a sign of a high-quality product. A high-quality vinyl floor like this might be the same price or even more expensive than a low- or medium-grade hardwood or wood laminate, but labor costs are lower than hardwood installation and the vinyl floor product will last longer.

JONATHAN: It isn't just flooring that has benefited from strides in technology. Electric fireplaces have improved drastically in style and function since the 1980s units that used lights, a mirror, and a fan to blow flame shaped fabric around a black box surrounded by a fake oak mantel. Today's high tech versions can use

evaporators and specialized lighting to achieve the realistic illusion of dancing flames and glowing embers. Most of these units include a built-in heat blower.

DREW: Jonathan knows all about blowing hot air. But did you know that electric fireplaces can be installed in places where it would be difficult or cost prohibitive to place a conventional wood burning or gas fireplace, such as in a master bedroom or bathroom, or on an interior wall? The newest electric fireplaces also come with a huge array of surrounds, from brushed stainless steel to hammered copper. They can look extremely modern or very traditional and offer tremendous flexibility. High-tech electric units can be more expensive than the dowdy, dated versions but they are still affordable and far less expensive than having a real wood-burning fireplace installed, which includes masonry work, a chimney, and exhaust systems. A high-end electric insert and

surround could cost from several hundred dollars to $2,000 to $3,000, whereas adding a wood burning or gas fireplace could cost upward of $10,000. In terms of resale, a sexy fireplace in nearly any room is a big plus. But do me a favor and don't run the cord and plug it in to the closest wall receptacle. This looks tacky. Hard wire the unit so that it feels properly built in.

JONATHAN: Countertops may not be as sexy as fireplaces, but counter material is another area where manmade or engineered products outpace natural stone in terms of appearance, durability, and maintenance. While granite has to be sealed every 6 to 12 months to prevent staining, and Carrara marble even more often, manmade counters, such as quartz, mimic natural stone and are virtually maintenance free. All you have to do is clean them.

DREW: The reason quartz never needs to be resealed is because it is made up of crushed quartz and resin. The resin actually seals the entire slab when it's manufactured. You can also get quartz slabs that look very similar to any stone slab you like—marble, granite, you name it! Other manmade products like NeoLith are also great because they never have to be resealed and can't be burned, stained, cut, or scuffed. NeoLith is basically a slab-style product similar to a robust porcelain tile, and it's easy to clean with a very modern look.

LIGHTING FIXTURES: Modern lighting fixtures go beyond traditional chandeliers, can lights, and plain ceiling fixtures. Today the options are almost limitless, making it easy to find a style that reinforces the overall look of your home.

FIREPLACES: The variety of fireplace styles is broad enough to suit every taste—from traditional to contemporary, country to urban.

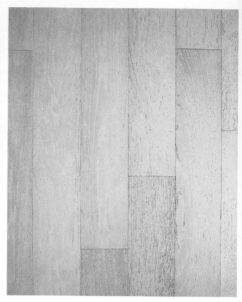

FLOORED! Can you tell the difference between laminate, real hardwood, and engineered hardwood? Technology has advanced so much that most people can't tell unless they get down on their hands and knees.

OPPOSITE, COUNTERTOPS: Concrete, stone, synthetic, and laminate—the choice of counter surfacing can be overwhelming. By determining the overall look and style you want to achieve in your kitchen or bath, you can narrow down your choices and get the right material to achieve the look you're after.

Good Grades

Most every building material and product has a variety of grades, and many brands manufacture more than one grade to give consumers a choice in price and quality. For most people, there is a sweet spot in terms of quality you can be safe with, and that's the mid-range. Sure, you can ship an exotic stone in from Italy, but you better love it because you will never get your money back on that investment. If you put really cheap materials in your house, you won't get good value for your own use, and you may have to replace them before you move. Replacing them with something just as cheap will not raise the price of your property, despite the fact that it's brand new. Cabinetry is one of the most common categories of graded products homeowners have to choose between. Here's a snapshot of the various product levels when dealing with cabinetry:

BUILDER-GRADE (AKA PREFAB STOCK):
Usually the least expensive product, because it has a minimum level of quality and is mass-produced. Builder-grade products, which you can often take right off the shelf in a big box home improvement store, are not bad, but they are basic—they come in a couple of sizes and a limited number of finishes. You often find builder-grade cabinetry in stock at big home centers. You can bring them home, and install in the same day. These cabinets take extra work to finish off nicely with crown and trim so that they don't look cheap. The average cost of all your prefab cabinets, moldings, panels, and hardware for a regular sized kitchen (about 15 cabinets, including uppers and lowers) would be under $5,000. You have to pay for installation and finishing on top of that. In general, you could add from $100 to $200 per box for installation, which means it could cost anywhere from $1,500 to $3,000 for installation. You can find builder-grade cabinets at big box home improvement stores or online that would cost even less, perhaps in the $2,000 to $2,500 range, but don't expect any long-lasting quality. In fact, if you buy the cheapest thing around, it may end up costing you more money because you will have to replace those cabinets sooner.

SEMI-CUSTOM: Semi-custom cabinets offer a range of styles and materials, including various wood species (maple, oak, birch, mahogany, etc.), color, special features, and options. Construction quality is better than builder-grade—for instance, drawers may have dovetailing instead of butt joints put together with glue and nails. You have much more control over the final product than you do with builder-grade, but without the cost custom-made cabinetry demands. Quality is somewhat comparable to custom, and you'll generally get a lot more sizing options than builder-grade. The downside of semi-custom is it can take as long as custom items to be manufactured and delivered—sometimes weeks or even months—depending on the manufacturer's schedule and demand. The average kitchen cost with semi-custom cabinets is about $10,000, and the manufacturer can usually offer reasonable rates for install.

CUSTOM: These are cabinets built for your specific space—sometimes on sight and sometimes in a workshop. Depending on who makes them, custom cabinets can be very expensive—even as high as $50,000 or more for labor and materials for a standard sized kitchen. We're not going to lie ... you can't beat the quality and customized solutions of a custom kitchen. Since every cabinet is made from scratch, they can be tailored to best use every square inch of the kitchen. You're paying for it, but you're getting life-long value in terms of function, aesthetics, and workmanship. But it's easy to start overspending, so be sure to do your research to know what buyers are willing to pay for in a kitchen reno. Even if it's your forever home, it's still smart to think of resale.

TILE STYLE: There are so many choices in tiles today, in terms of both looks and materials. From porcelain and stone to glass and synthetic or manmade materials, tiles offer a lot of design opportunities and applications. There are companies that allow you to design custom made tiles, or mix and match colors and patterns, at an affordable price, especially if you are judicious about their use.

Steals and Deals

We are never opposed to bargain shopping for home improvement products. We only caution that price alone does not make a great deal. Know where to go and what you're buying before you lay down cash. Shows like *Property Brothers* and *Buying and Selling* have spoiled the public to a certain extent (we admit it!); it's really window shopping from your TV. Then you have to go out and find the product or something similar based on what you've seen. Consumers know a lot more about what's available these days than they used to, and it goes way beyond what they see at the local home center. There is a way to find the special fixtures and materials you want without spending a fortune. Here are some ideas:

CLASSIFIED ADS: Scouring Craigslist and other online classified ads and community bulletin boards can be a great way to find materials, especially salvaged items. We worked with a homeowner who scored a $12,000 like-new Wolf appliance package on Craigslist for $1,000. The sellers were completely overhauling their kitchen and starting from scratch, and they just wanted to move the three-year-old appliances out of the house. Our clients were ready and able to pay for the premium professional brand of appliances with cash and take them away the same day. The homeowner inspected everything and found them to be in working condition. That deal saved thousands of dollars in appliance costs, money that could go back into the homeowners' pocket, or be used to upgrade other finishes and fixtures. We know of people who have bought like-new kitchen cabinets for next to nothing from homeowners who were doing renovations. For something like cabinets, you just need to make sure they will work with your kitchen layout.

Only buy items like this if they are in great shape and you like them—it's not a bargain if what you're buying isn't really what you want. We worked with another couple who thought they had found a great deal on flooring via a classified ad, but a quick inspection revealed that the wood floor was low quality and wouldn't last. In other words, it was cheap because it was cheap. You also need to keep in mind that many products online, especially used, may not have a warranty. For something like appliances, you really want to kick the tires prior to purchasing.

AUCTIONS: Going to auctions can be a bit more time-consuming than conventional retail shopping, but it's also a lot of fun and can be great for scoring bargains. Local auctions sell all sorts of things, including perfectly usable building supplies, appliances, furniture, and fixtures. In the U.S., plug your zip code into the Auctionzip.com search engine to find auctions near you, including pictures and descriptions of the items that are going to be up for sale. If you're in a time crunch, auctions may not be the best way to score building materials because they are pretty unpredictable, and you might have to wait a while before finding the perfect tile for your bathroom. However, auctions are great sources for character pieces, such as unique vintage lighting fixtures, artwork, and architectural details like columns or fireplace mantels and surrounds that make your renovation truly one-of-a-kind and custom. Often these items can be "won" for a fraction of their retail price. P.S.: If you've never been to an auction, don't raise your number until the auctioneer brings down the opening bid to a number lower than you can live with, and set a limit as to when to put your paddle down. You have to do your research to know the going price for the products or materials you're looking to pick up. It's the same at an auction as when you are buying a home. If you've done your research you'll be sure not to get swept up in the excitement of the moment and pay more than products are actually worth.

FLOOR MODELS AND END RUNS: Don't be afraid to negotiate the price of floor models at retail stores, especially on appliances, furnishings, and limited tile and flooring stock. Management wants to move the items out of the store, so they have some incentive and leeway to work on the asking price. When buying "scratch and dent" appliances make sure the aesthetics and functionality aren't compromised by whatever damage may have been done to the piece. We've picked up a $1,200 range for $550 because of a dent, *but* the damage was actually on the side of the appliance, which would be hidden by the cabinets. Sometimes it's minor, but other times, a dent in the wrong place could (and probably should) be a deal breaker. When buying discontinued or end runs of flooring or tiling material, make sure you buy enough for your application plus 10 percent, for cuts and what we call *attic stock,* in case you need to replace or repair the material at some point in the future. It's pretty much impossible to find discontinued materials after the fact, so again, if you can't buy enough of what you need for a project; that's not a bargain.

MIXING HIGH AND LOW: We often do this, especially in kitchens and bathrooms. For instance, instead of tiling your shower with expensive marble or glass mosaic pieces, opt for a *ground* (or *field*) of simple white subway tiles or a neutral porcelain tile, adding the expensive tiles in a detail such as a band. Buy stock cabinets and customize them with crown molding, or remove the doors of two cabinets to create open shelving, another custom look. Do a less expensive butcher-block countertop on your island, and then splurge on a beautiful composite or stone surface for the rest of your counters. You achieve the same impact and look as you would if you had gone all the way with the expensive material—but at a fraction of what it would have cost you.

SEASONAL SALES: Just as January is a traditional time to put bedding and linens on sale, home improvement items are also part of retailers' regular sale cycles. If the timing is right, you can score great buys on things you need right at your local home improvement center. Check the sale calendar opposite for a year's worth of home improvement sales. Note that some items come up for sales more than once a year—giving you more options to get deals on what you need throughout the year. For anything surrounding outdoor entertainment, patio, or landscaping, shop in the late fall and winter months for the best deals. For any winter related, weather proofing, heating, etc., shop early summer. The deals are just waiting to be found!

HOME RENO STEALS AND DEALS RETAIL CALENDAR

January
- Air conditioners
- Carpeting and flooring
- Furniture
- Gas grills
- Linens and bedding

February
- Home theaters
- Electronics
- Outdoor furniture
- Indoor furniture
- Bathroom fixtures and cabinetry

March
- Flowering plants and bulbs
- Outdoor furniture
- Small appliances

April
- Televisions and other electronics
- Cookware and kitchen accessories
- Vacuum cleaners
- Lawn mowers

May
- Refrigerators
- Mattresses
- Office furniture
- Outdoor gear
- Lawn mowers
- Small appliances

June
- Dishware
- Tools
- Indoor furniture
- Small appliances

July
- Furniture
- Home décor
- Tools
- Outdoor furniture

August
- Linens
- Storage containers
- Computers
- Air conditioners
- Dehumidifiers
- Snow blowers
- Outdoor furniture

September
- Appliances
- Lawn mowers
- Shrubs, trees, and perennials
- Snow blowers
- Small appliances and electronics

October
- Appliances
- Patio and other outdoor furniture
- Cookware and kitchen accessories
- Gas grills and air conditioners
- Plants

November
- Appliances
- Televisions and other electronics
- Tools
- Gas grills

December
- Pools
- Televisions and other electronics
- Tools
- Gas grills
- Large and small home appliances

"REALTY" CHECK: TECHNOLOGY IS BEAUTIFUL

Stainless steel is still the popular default appliance finish among homeowners; however, as design and engineering improves and develops, that's changing. Don't feel you have to choose stainless when renovating a kitchen. More manufacturers are creating interesting finishes in white, black, and other colors, including white glass-paneled appliances and enamel-look finishes that evoke a retro look but are classic and high-end. If you want to stick with stainless, rest assured that appliance makers have developed the finish to a point where the fingerprint mark issue has largely been resolved. Not that either of us ever have sticky fingers!

Technology is becoming more and more integrated into appliance panels too: Refrigerators have televisions, computers, and electronic memo boards on door panels. Glass countertops allow you to check your email and do web searches for recipes. Computers and technology vanish into countertops, cabinet doors, and the refrigerator. Tablets enable you to control multiple systems, including climate, music, video, home security, and lighting. Technology grows exponentially, so expect high-tech features to become more affordable and most likely standard in appliances and fixtures over the next few years.

It's already happening in the bathroom. Digital shower controls let you preset preferred temperature, water volume, and massage settings. If you don't like what you see in the mirror, you can turn on the TV and look at us! Integrated televisions are going to become common in your bathroom mirror as a way to get your morning news ... or catch up on Hollywood gossip. Kohler's Numi toilet has a motion activated cover and seat; integrated air dryer; deodorizer; seat warmer; foot warmer; and music. Sensor faucets for bathrooms reduce the spread of germs and minimize water usage—clean and green! Jetted tub technology has also improved. It used to be a chore to clean out the jets. In fact, we had a client who developed a rash from bathing in a tub with dirty jets. Yes, disgusting. Today air jets eliminate the problem of grime and mold buildup.

New finishes in appliances give stainless steel some attractive competition.

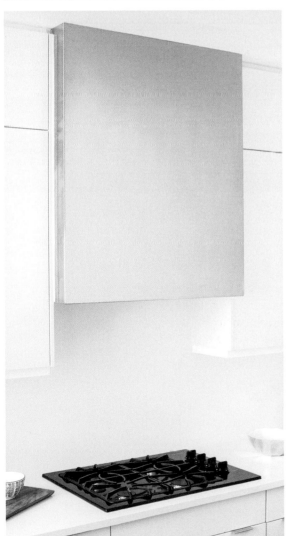

Technology has brought the World Wide Web into every room in the house—now via countertops, mirrors, and appliance doors.

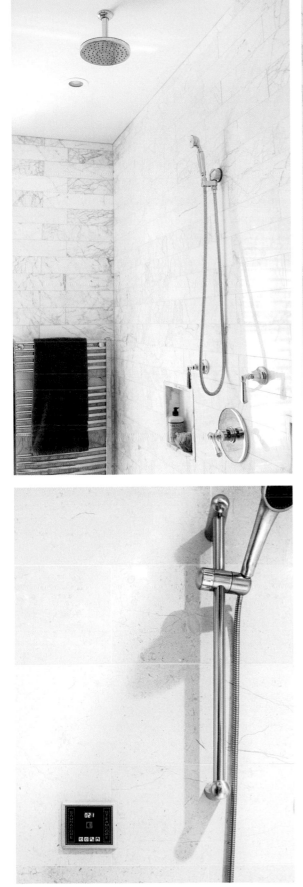

Digital shower controls and
rain showerheads are just
some of the features that bring
bathrooms into the 21st century.

INVISIBLE BENEFITS OF GREEN
And Efficient Materials

Home building materials aren't limited to the pretty stuff you see on the surface. There are plenty of items that work behind the scenes and in out-of-the-way places that make your home more livable. Obviously, reclaimed material, such as timber, is very green and clean. Recycled-content materials are made from the stuff collected in recycling programs around the country. So whenever you're tempted to toss the plastic bottles or paper in the trash instead of the recycling barrel, don't do it! These items are used to make brand new, sustainable products. So please ask your contractor to look for insulation that is made at least partially from recycled goods.

Drywall can use recycled paper and post-industrial gypsum board. Many insulation products reuse cellulose, mineral wool, fiberglass, and recycled cotton insulation. Lumber (including molding and trim) can be made from recycled plastic, and it looks like the real thing. Many beams are made from either recycled or composite wood that has been laminated together to create light, but incredibly strong, support systems. Many beams are also made from recycled steel. Landscaping materials, including long-lasting mulch, can be made from post-use plastics. Products made from recycled content are usually labeled with percentages of postconsumer and recovered material. If an item is labeled *recycled* it has to contain used, rebuilt, reconditioned, or remanufactured parts, unless it's obvious to the consumer, such as when you buy something marked "used" at a resale shop like Habitat for Humanity's ReStore. We donate as much used material as we can to Habitat for Humanity, whether it's cabinets, flooring, or something else. But remember, if the item has seen better days and it'll cost money to repair, it may not be worth the headache of donating.

Money- and energy-saving products are always worth the investment, not only for your own bills but for resale too. Yes, buyers do look for, and are attracted to, green and economical heating and cooling systems, energy efficient windows and insulation, and even smart lighting systems. Some of these products qualify for government tax credits and rebates when used in a renovation, so check with manufacturers for this perk. Over time, efficient systems save money on utility bills too.

For instance, an on-demand hot water system can substantially reduce energy use by only heating water when you need it. Otherwise your old tank is heating up the entire volume of water every hour or so … whether or not you use it. There are some hybrid systems that have a small tank inside them, and the rest is on demand, offering the best of both worlds. No cold blast when you run the water, yet still unlimited hot water when you need it.

The newest air conditioner units are far more efficient than the big monsters from the past. You might consider switching out ugly window AC units with slim wall units that almost disappear in the room. However, keep in mind that while a central air conditioning system is more expensive to retrofit into a home that does not have one, and wall units are less expensive up front, central air conditioners are more efficient than room air conditioners. Today's efficient air conditioning systems use 30 to 50 percent less energy to produce the same amount of cooling as air conditioners made in the 1970s. An efficient unit bought today will save between 20 and 40 percent of cooling costs compared to a unit made just 10 years ago!

Radiant heating systems installed under flooring are best if they operate via hot water. These floors are very efficient to run, but initially costly to install, between $5,000 and $15,000 to retrofit a home. Most of the cost is from the labor involved with taking up flooring and then putting it back once the installation is complete. But if you are taking out flooring as part of a renovation, adding in-floor heating is a safe bet. Heated floors are a cost effective way to keep things cozy, but if you want the comfort without the expense of a whole-room system, install the system in a smaller area. For instance, in-floor heating is handy around the kitchen sink, in an entryway, or in the bathroom. Who doesn't love stepping into their master bathroom and feeling warmth instead of the shock of cold tile—yes, even in the desert? Over time, radiant systems do pay for themselves in terms of energy savings.

Old, inefficient windows can be thermal black holes. An average home can lose a whopping 30 percent of its heat or air-conditioning energy through inefficient windows. Energy-efficient windows save money every month, and can actually reduce noise transfer too—and all you see is the beautiful new window. The cost to replace far outweighs the improved comfort, upgraded aesthetics, and quiet acoustics. You may be eligible for a government-sponsored rebate if you replace old windows with efficient new ones. Current U.S. guidelines say that homeowners can receive a tax credit equal to 10 percent of the product cost (not including the installation cost) up to $200 for eligible windows and $500 for eligible doors. Eligibility requirements vary depending on the region of the country you live in and are available from energystar.gov.

FEATHERING YOUR NEST

DESIGN AND DÉCOR

Once the dust has settled and your renovation is complete, the fun of "dressing" the rooms in a way that expresses your personality begins. It sounds great, doesn't it? Except that for a lot of people—maybe you—this also happens to be when design paralysis sets in. Magazines and television shows make it look so easy, but when you attempt interior design on your own, the fear of making a mistake, or actually making a mistake, is palpably scary. After all, furniture, lighting, and accessories represent a major expense, so mistakes can be costly. Most homeowners tell us they can't envision how furniture and textiles will work together when they see them individually as samples. Instead they throw up their hands and give up. Or, they take their cues from home store catalogs, where everything looks so pristine and neat, and they end up with something generic looking and devoid of character! A well-designed room should look as if it's been curated over time, not shipped right from the warehouse.

Inspiration boards are great tools for keeping track of ideas, color schemes, fabric swatches, paint chips, samples, materials, and even cards with names and numbers of vendors. After you finish designing your room, keep the board as a reference when you're ready to swap out pieces or add new ones in.

BY DESIGN:
Create a Personal Home

You can't just throw all your old stuff back into a new space and expect it to "work," nor is it likely that you can afford to entirely refurnish your pad. You've probably collected pieces specifically for the new space, but keep in mind you don't have to "clean house" and get rid of all the old. We usually reuse up to 50 percent of a client's existing furniture and décor. Some of it needs to be refinished, and some reupholstered. Take a look around and plan to keep some old favorites. You most likely need new shades for every window in the house, as well as some soft furnishings (pillows, throws, drapes), lamps and lighting, artwork, accents, and other decorative accessories to fill out your rooms to give them personality. Coordinating furniture, rugs, and paint adds more layers of design madness. It can be overwhelming, even for a pro. If you're dealing with family members who have different tastes and who want to express them in your home's décor, you will have even more challenges. When we were decorating our Las Vegas house, we disagreed on the design direction and many details. Ultimately, Drew took control of some of the spaces, and Jonathan took charge of others—there's no one right way to design rooms (although Jonathan insists the right way is simply his way).

ABOVE: A dark round Victorian style pedestal table is set off by a modern rustic chandelier and contemporary, light-colored chairs.

RIGHT: A traditional fireplace gets a burst of energy from modern, clean-lined furnishings.

OPPOSITE: A modern headboard sets off vintage nightstands.

We both have confidence in our sense of style (see page 255), but with larger scale projects and especially balancing up to nine projects at a time, we still enlist the help of other professional interior designers whom we trust to carry out the fine details according to Jonathan's design. Getting pros on board is crucial with any project, and even more so on television where we're always under the pressure (make that threat!) of tight schedules and deadlines. You've probably noticed everything on the show gets done about three times faster than you'd ever be able to do it. Well, those are all real timelines … so trust us, the pros we have working with us are the best.

For those of you not being followed around by a camera crew as you place abstract pictures in a living room, you can still feel pressured to get it right and get it done on time. But if you have the luxury of living in the space for a while, do so and get a feel for the style you want to develop in each room.

An interior designer is like any other pro in that a good one makes your life easier, saves you from making costly mistakes, and, especially in this case, literally makes your house (and you) look good. Like a general contractor, a designer can organize and manage the entire project, keeping it on task and on budget, and is your point person whenever you have a question or concern. He can catch problems and nip them in the bud before they cause big problems. Quite often, the products that show up from manufacturers are damaged in shipping, or not exactly what was ordered, so the designer will know what items are wrong and either return them or fix them so they work.

Contractors, as talented and important as they are, are usually not interior designers. They're great at following a plan, having an eye for detail, and executing a design, but generally don't have the same experience in conceptualizing all the finer elements that need to come together to create the perfect space. Design is not just about the studs and the drywall. It's also about how the space is styled and gets to that move-in-ready state. Sure, a contractor can tear down a wall to give you open concept, just as a cabinetmaker will figure out the right size cabinets for your kitchen, but as far as making the key aesthetics decisions for a space to work, you need an interior designer. A designer will create a smart floor plan and ensure the textures, colors, and both hard and soft furnishings work together throughout the entire home, and within the overall floor plan. He can also source unique décor pieces and furnishings from "industry professional only" sources, items you would never be able to get at retail stores, or pieces you just don't have the time to find at auctions, flea markets, and estate sales.

Don't let the idea of hiring an interior designer put you off because of the perceived high cost. Of course there are very elite interior designers who cater to high-end clients with very few price barriers, but the majority of interior designers work with all kinds of clients, budgets, and styles.

SIX WAYS TO PAY
An Interior Designer

According to the American Society of Interior Designers (ASID), there are six common ways designers work, one or more of which is sure to suit your needs. Remember your designer can do as little as help you decide on a color palette and design furniture layout, or as much as handle the entire project right down to purchasing all the furniture and décor pieces, even cabinet handles, and installing them in the home. The more they do, the more they cost. Go figure?

1. A FIXED OR FLAT FEE agreement is where the designer specifies a sum that will cover costs, not including expenses. This fee applies to the complete scope of services proposed, from conceptual development through layouts, specifications, and final installation.

2. HOURLY FEES are based on the actual time that the designer consults on a project. This is a very flexible way to go, as you can call in an hourly designer to take charge of a specific room or service. Generally speaking, the smaller the project is, the higher the hourly rate will be (many designers have a minimum fee, even when charging a hourly rate). For example, a designer may charge $150 an hour, with a minimum of four hours.

3. PERCENTAGE OF PROJECT FEE is computed as a percentage markup on the total project cost, including furnishings and services purchased or specified on behalf of a client. This can often range anywhere from 10 percent to 30 percent, depending on how much work is involved, and where you live (a New York City designer may charge more than one in Brunswick, Maine, for example).

4. A RETAINER is what a client pays up front for ongoing design services on an open-ended project. This is where a client often hires a designer for an unspecified period of time and the designer brings ideas and items to the client for his or her approval.

5. COST PLUS is when a designer charges a percentage on top of the cost of specified materials, furnishings that the designer has bought at wholesale prices. Regardless of whether the designer gets an item at wholesale or below, they usually bill the retail rate. This should be discussed with the client in advance but if you think about it, as a regular Joe you'd be paying retail anyway, so it's not out of line. If they are marking up to retail, plus charging a percentage, then there usually isn't a management fee too. However, some designers will pass the savings on to you on things they buy at wholesale prices. Once again, discuss and then get the terms in writing. If a designer has a website, these terms are often explained in detail there.

6. A PER SQUARE FOOT CHARGE, perhaps the least common payment style, is when the designer charges fees based on the square footage of the project. This isn't our favorite method as we find it to be the least accurate.

If you've never used an interior designer before and you are on a really, really tight budget, we recommend starting out with one on a consulting basis so you only have to pay hourly for the work they have done. Perhaps just have the designer help you identify a "look" or style, lay out the floor plan, find paint colors, and identify key pieces, like sofas, area rugs, and décor. Then you can implement everything they have suggested. It's more work for you but it costs far less and gives you a chance to see if you really like working with the person without committing to a major investment of time and money. It also gives you an opportunity to be involved with the design process, which is key in getting exactly what you want. However, there are clients, often on the higher end of the cost spectrum, who have a long term relationship with a designer and trust him or her to create a room without consultation.

FIGURE OUT
What You Like

We advocate creating some sort of inspiration board or notebook—a place to pin or post photographs of furnishings you like or simply inspiration for colors, textures, textiles, and so on. You can create an actual board (see one of ours on page 238), or use our *Property Brothers* app or a scrapbook-like site such as Pinterest. When we work with homeowners on our shows, we show them tons of pictures to get a really good idea of their sense of style. They point to what they like and, sometimes even more important, what they don't like—it's the best way to start so we can really get a handle on what their color and style preferences are. Often they surprise themselves because they'll point out something that they had never considered before, or even realized they would ever be attracted to. What we've found is that most homeowners don't really know what they like … until we show it to them. So we're always willing to take some risks.

The best thing you can do, as an untrained homeowner, is beg, borrow, and steal every design idea that you like. Go to a real paint store where the staff is trained and ask questions about paint grades, finishes, and color. Paint store employees know what goes into the colors, and many large chains even have free apps that will color match or pick palettes for you. For instance, they can tell you which yellows are created with a warmer base and which aren't, or which color would look best in a darker kitchen or a basement. Maybe you're overwhelmed with the thought that there are over a thousand shades of gray? How on earth do you know what would look better in an office setting or perhaps a basement den? All of this is easy for a professional designer, but even if you're working with one, you can't completely check out of the decision process because picking the right color is always a delicate balance of design and personal preference, so you still play an integral role.

Regardless of what kind of project you're doing, you can get inspiration from images from our website or app, and also websites such as Houzz.com, Google Images, and DesignSponge.com—the possible sources for inspiration are endless. Spend a couple of hours browsing through magazines and online decorating sites, and you'll start to notice a common theme or "look" that feels right for you. Don't be afraid to try something new and definitely take notes on what makes you say, "Yes! I love it," and what makes you think to yourself, "No way."

DESIGN IS PART OF YOUR BUDGET

Everything you see in the spaces on *Property Brothers* was worked into the overall reno budget and stays in the house unless the homeowners remove it after we leave. Our budget for décor is based on the assumption that we'll use up to 50 percent of the homeowner's possessions, either as is or repurposed, restored, or transformed in some way. It's a smart way to proceed, since the costs of furniture and décor can sneak up on you and bite you in, uh, your wallet. Even the work we plan to do on existing furnishings is part of the budget. It's often not until an hour or so past the reveal that a homeowner realizes, "Hey wait ... oh yeah, that *is* my old sofa, but they reupholstered it," or, "That's my dining table, but it looks completely new and different because it's been painted."

We even fit custom-look drapes into the often-tight budgets. We've gone to Ikea for simple white panels (less than $10 each) and then to the fabric store for some interesting drapery material. We use that material to create a 10- or 12-inch band for either the top or the bottom of the drape, and the result looks like an expensive, customized window treatment.

KEEP WHAT'S GOOD,
Lose What's Awful

Keep in mind that while your family heirlooms, antiques, and vintage items *can* be renewed, repurposed, and reused, the transformation will be successful only if they are appealing in some way and in solid shape to begin with. It's not worth the money in the long run to repair something that isn't that valuable, or to renew it if it doesn't have "good bones." Most people's antiques are not going to turn out to be their retirement nest egg.

You might have a mid-century modern table that's in solid shape with great lines, but a dodgy finish. By stripping, sanding, and re-staining it, you can breathe fresh life into it. It's worth the effort. But fixing up and reupholstering a 1980s floral sofa is not a good idea if it's structurally unsound. In that situation, you're better off buying a new couch.

Many people we work with have finite budgets, so the idea of repurposing pieces and extending the memories of where they came from is very appealing. Some homeowners say to us there is *no* way we can paint over this sideboard, as it was a gift from their grandmother. Oh come on … Grandma would not want you to have something awful in your house. She'd love you to fix up that old sideboard and be proud of it. We have proven this time and time again on *Property Brothers*. If you don't want to refinish it, then sell it and put the money toward something that *does* work with your design. In other words, be brutally honest with yourself about your stuff. Donate or Craigslist the crappy flat-pack furniture, anything broken or downright ugly (you *know* what we're talking about), or simply out of sync with your space's new personality. It doesn't matter if you spent $2,500 on a reclining sofa with vibrating cushions in 1985. It's the 21st century … it's time to let it go!

BROTHER VS. BROTHER:

Style Rivals

JONATHAN: My aesthetic is best expressed through a mix of furnishings and natural materials with pops of color—it has a collected feeling. It's contemporary but classic in the sense that it won't be out of style next year. It's an easy look to tweak and update because it's not beholden to a strict style vernacular. I coined the term *elegantly eclectic* to describe it. I love incorporating conversation pieces into my designs, things I've picked up from travels—so there's a story behind each one. Or, maybe I just love to throw a wrench in the works to create something more interesting. (I do actually have antique wrenches that I have used as décor.)

DREW: My taste is much more modern and clean-lined than Jonathan's. I love geometric shapes that reference the iconic, modern silhouettes of the mid-20th century period. I'm not at all opposed to vintage pieces, if they are original examples of modern classics, like Arne Jacobsen's Swan Chair or a Le Corbusier sofa. I like to feature some of these character pieces without having too many of them because I feel it takes away from the sleek, modern style that I love. I don't want my rooms to look like museums. They have to be clean, comfortable, and inviting ... oh, and have *lots* of shoe storage.

JONATHAN: We agree, however, when it comes to having a minimalist feel in our spaces. Neither of us likes clutter or objects that don't either serve a purpose or meet a very high design standard. If something feels out of place or overbearing, it's gone.

DREW: And of course it's fun to have a signature piece in a room, something specific to you that references your interests or hobbies.

JONATHAN: Yes, I like to sneak in an owl or some tartan into every client's project. I don't tell them. I just do it. Shhh.

DREW: Really? I just think, "This isn't his house, what if they don't like the owls and tartan?"

JONATHAN: How could you not like a cute little owl ... or a kilt?

INCORPORATE
Old Pieces with New

A successful room is all in the mix. Here are some specific ideas to get you started:

> Hang a modern chandelier over a wide-plank, country-style dining table.

> Use a contemporary reclaimed wood coffee table to anchor more traditional upholstered armchairs.

> Add leather Moroccan "poufs" to an ultra-modern room for some ethnic-inspired seating.

> Give a traditional sofa and chairs a burst of energy with a very sleek steel and glass coffee table.

> Use a round rustic-looking fixture with exposed Edison bulbs to highlight a dark round Victorian-style pedestal table and upholstered dining chairs with Tudor-inspired legs in a lighter wood tone.

> Contrast a Louis-style settee by giving it a modern touch with a coat of bright aqua blue paint.

> Offset a modern headboard with two vintage nightstands.

THERE'S AN APP FOR THAT

There are so many apps to help you track, organize, and design your rooms, and some even check what a room would look like with a certain color on the walls. Here are a few of our favorites:

> Surprise, surprise, our own Property Brothers app (available soon!) offers tips and tricks on how to budget, manage, and carry out your project. There are tons of photos and videos, and you can even create your own mood board.

> HGTV's free Shelf app offers advice from the network's cadre of experts, before and after slideshows, and video clips from popular shows.

> Neat works on Android and iOS phones and lets you scan receipts, paint chips, and business cards with your phone—for free. Then, for a fee, you can use the app to search those digital files on Neat's secure cloud.

> Yes, there are plenty of apps that allow you lay out a room. Some allow you to virtually insert furniture and arrange and rearrange it with advice from an interior designer. For instance, Ikea has free room design software you can use to arrange furniture in a room. Unfortunately the 3D designs we do on our shows are *way* too expensive for consumer use, so we recommend finding one of these inexpensive solutions.

TELL A COMPELLING
Color Story

There's no need to get stuck on boring beige walls and white trim. Have a little fun with color. Here's our foolproof formula for creating a color palette that gives life and interest to your rooms but still achieves a pleasing flow and connection between spaces in your home.

1. Choose three colors pulled from either a fabric or wallpaper in the main room of your house.

2. From each of these three colors, choose three shades in various intensities: dark, medium, and light.

3. Add in a neutral white, cream, or off-white that works with the three color families you have selected.

4. Choose one of your light intensity tones for the walls of the room, and then use the medium intensities for floor coverings or possibly some furniture pieces. The brightest or darkest intensity tones can be used as accents.

Wallpaper in a bold geometric pattern has traditional roots, but is youthful and fun.

LOOKS GREAT
On Paper!

Wallpaper is one of those things that most people either absolutely love or passionately hate. The haters tend to be the ones who have tried to remove it. Yet, if chosen carefully and not done in excess, wallpaper adds great impact, texture, and color to a space, and for that reason, we often use it on an accent wall in a bedroom or common area. Any room can support the use of wallpaper, even kitchens and bathrooms, if you choose wisely. In this instance, less is definitely more. Today there are many modern options that are totally original or take inspiration from traditional patterns, but play with scale and color in modern ways. Vintage papers can also provide a unique touch in small doses, such as the back lining for open shelving, to dress up an alcove, reading or breakfast nook, or even to freshen up a staircase. We have come across some terrible uses of wallpaper on *Property Brothers*, many so bad that we just had to tweet them. A couple of simple rules from our experience: Do not line every surface in a room with wallpaper, do not have naked characters in the pattern, don't use wallpaper as a shower surround, and farm animals and cats are a no-no. Yes, we've seen all of these. Here are some quick tips when choosing wallpaper for the rooms in your house:

> **BATHROOM:** A bold or whimsical pattern is an excellent choice for a bathroom because it creates an interesting juxtaposition between the small size of most bathrooms and the large scale of the pattern. It's also unexpected—making it the perfect choice for a guest bath or main floor powder room.

> **BEDROOM:** Think relaxation. A tone-on-tone pattern, subtle damask, or a paper that features a soft, abstract take on natural themes, like leaves, branches, birds or flowers, can be soothing and pretty. Just be careful not to choose anything that is too busy or bold or that will give you vertigo when you enter the room. Wallpaper should be a beautiful accent but not distracting to the overall design.

> **LIVING ROOM:** Bold geometrics and stripes can pull together a modern or retro mid-century room, catapulting it right into the 21st century. Look for muted shades, or the use of matte and gloss, to create a one-color pattern.

> **KITCHEN:** Refrain from getting too thematic—pass up the mixed fruit or wine bottle border prints. Instead, go for a modern interpretation, like a sunny yellow or orange grass cloth below a chair rail or a very graphic pattern that references food and nature in a more subtle and abstract way.

OPPOSITE: Wallpaper in a bathroom? Why not? In a small space you can go with something bold and whimsical.

STILL AFRAID OF WALLPAPER?

How about a large-scaled vintage schoolhouse or typographical map?
Attach it to a board and finish it off with picture frame molding. It makes
a bold graphic (and educational) statement, but it's also easily removed.

A muted plaid feature wall in this bedroom is masculine but softened by touches of lucite and sparkling chrome. We all know Jonathan loves this!

IT ALL ADDS UP
To Great Design

Achieving a pleasing sense of proportion and scale in a room isn't all that complicated actually—if you have a tape measure. Many times, getting the numbers right is all it takes. Here are some common measurement guidelines that are sure to bring some aesthetic harmony to your house:

AREA RUGS

› The distance between an area rug and at least one wall should be between 12 and 18 inches so that flooring is visible. In oversized great rooms you can increase that distance between wall and rug or have it completely free floating in the center of the room if the space is big enough.

› The front legs of your sofa and chairs should sit on an area rug—ideally the entire furniture grouping should be within the perimeter of an area rug.

ARMCHAIRS

› A pair of armchairs should sit about one foot apart in a seating arrangement, or two feet apart with a side table in between.

ART AND MIRRORS

› Leave 2 inches between frames when hanging artwork or mirrors in groupings.

› 60 inches to the base is the optimal height for hanging larger pictures and mirrors on walls without other architectural features. We find most people hang their art too low. It should be in the upper one-third of an unobstructed wall.

CHANDELIERS AND HANGING FIXTURES

› Leave about 66 inches from the floor to the bottom of a dining table fixture. This leaves enough room for a centerpiece and doesn't block the sight lines of people at the table—but it still leaves the table well lit.

› For rectangular tables longer than 6 feet, an elongated fixture or two chandeliers may be necessary.

COFFEE TABLES

› Most sofa seats are 17 to 20 inches high, so an adjacent coffee table should be 15 to 18 inches high. Perfect height for putting your feet up ... not that our mom encourages that.

> Allow around 18 inches between the coffee table and sofa edge to provide comfortable legroom—that's close enough to set down drinks or reach snacks without straining or getting up.

DINING TABLE AND CHAIRS

> Try to provide at least 36 inches between the dining table and any walls or other furniture on all sides to allow seats to slide out easily and people to sit down without twisting an arm or an ankle.

> Chairs and chair arms should be able to slide under a table easily. Allow for several inches between the chair arm and apron of the table.

> Place dining chairs 6 inches apart *at an absolute minimum,* to prevent diners from colliding with one another.

HEADBOARDS

> The standard height of a headboard is 48 inches from the floor to its top, which leaves about 24 inches from the top of the mattress to the top of the headboard. Higher end headboards tend to be 55 to 68 inches, which works much better for us as we are tall. You want it to be comfortable enough to lean back against and read this book. Be careful about hanging artwork above the headboard, as you want to ensure you won't knock your head on it.

> You can go higher if you have the ceiling height. Just be sure to balance a high headboard with mattress-height nightstands (anything lower looks wonky). We personally prefer padded or tufted headboards, as they are comfortable to sit up against in bed.

NIGHTSTANDS

> Leave 2 inches between your nightstand and your bed—easy enough to reach for a glass or water or the alarm clock.

> The ideal nightstand depth is 25 inches or less—any deeper and you might hurt your shoulder when rolling out of bed!

> Think about scale. The larger the bed, the bigger your nightstand can go. King sized beds have the heft to stand up to a two-door cabinet, a three-drawer dresser, or even a drop-leaf table—if you've got the space go for it. For a twin or double bed, "leggy" tables and narrow three-drawer dressers (no more than 24 to 32 inches wide) work best.

> Don't worry too much about matching the nightstands—sometimes it's more interesting to choose two styles that contrast but complement each other.

"REALTY" CHECK: SOME OF OUR FAVORITE THINGS

You may have noticed that we have a few other signature items we love to bring into rooms, aside from Jonathan's tartan and owls. These classic pieces seem to work with a variety of styles and add color and/or light to a room. Maybe some of them will inspire you too.

1. GEOMETRIC PRINT FABRICS AND PAPERS: Fun and modern, geometrics work especially well in shared spaces because they are not obviously feminine, nor are they ultra-masculine. Use fabric for accent pillows, or frame fabric swatches; use wallpaper samples for instant artwork, or paper one wall of a room for a bold accent.

---

2. MIRRORED SIDE TABLES: They reflect light and bring a little bling even to more rustic spaces.

---

3. SEE-THROUGH SHELVING UNITS: They are functional and very sculptural—they also act as space dividers without blocking too much light. They are perfect for storing collectibles.

4. SLIDING BARN DOORS:
They are both rustic and industrial looking—depending on the finish and the hardware used to mount them to the wall. Sliding barn doors serve other purposes as well—as a design idea they're unique and textural, and they're also functional by closing off openings between rooms (or not) without taking up floor space.

5. VINTAGE TRUNK AS COFFEE TABLE: These well-traveled pieces double as storage and add history to a room.

6. PAINTED FURNITURE: Even a classic Louis-style sofa or very traditional ottoman can take on a whole new and modern, family-friendly life with a bright coat of gloss or semi-gloss paint.

7. INDUSTRIAL PIECES: We love re-purposing industrial furnishings and fixtures for residential use, whether it's a set of 1950s metal lockers, a 1940s steel desk, or an open wire-guard ceiling light. These elements add texture and a funky vintage feel even in hyper-modern or super-traditional rooms.

Create "zones" in open spaces through strategically placed furniture. Here, stools at the island eliminate the need for an "eat-in" kitchen table. Instead, a desk and chair near cabinetry create a functional office space—but the storage keeps clutter at bay.

PLOT OUT THE
Right Plan

Whether you use graph paper, a digital floor plan app, or just brute strength to move furniture around a room until you get it right, there are some basics for creating the most welcoming rooms, both public spaces for socializing and personal spaces for feeling comfortable when retreating from the world alike.

> **MAXIMIZE FOCAL POINTS.** The best way to lay out a space is to understand the features of the room and direct people to them. Arrange furniture to complement, rather than fight or compete with, the focal point in your room. If the view is spectacular, then orient furniture groupings near windows to encourage people to sit and take it in. If a stunning fireplace or art display draws the eye, arrange furnishings so when seated, guests can enjoy them.

> **ZONE OUT.** Create multiple functional areas in large rooms—in a living room that means more than one seating area, perhaps one that takes in a view and another centered on a game table or a television. In a bedroom, consider creating an area for sleeping and another for reading or working on a hobby.

> **LEAVE ROOM TO MOVE.** People need to come in and out of a room without trouble, sit down without straining, and socialize without shouting (unless you want them to—and why would that be?). Make sure there's enough space to move around in the room—if that means getting rid of some pieces, do not be afraid to edit.

> **VARY SCALE AND HEIGHT.** Don't let a room get overwhelmed by furnishings of the same scale or "heft." Instead, vary the shape and size of items so that your eye moves around the room, stopping to pause for a rest before moving on.

GLORIOUS OUTDOORS

GREEN SPACES FOR PLANTS AND PEOPLE

We're rarely able to talk about outdoor spaces on our shows, even though yards and gardens are such an important aspect of a home. We even designed a line of outdoor furniture and accessories for our Scott Living collection. However, for our shows, we focus on the areas of the home that are most important to those specific homeowners, and it just so happens that many of them choose kitchens, bathrooms, family rooms, and bedrooms. When we do have a chance to get our hands dirty (well, when Jonathan gets his hands dirty and Drew watches from the patio with a margarita in hand), we love to put our personal touch on a yard. When we buy our own houses to improve and then sell them, we never neglect landscaping since the front scape is the first impression anyone will have of the home and the backyard is typically a perfect area for those long awaited staycations.

Our Las Vegas property had a house ... and that was it. The rest of the half-acre lot was just dirt. We wanted to maximize the usable space and therefore decided to create several defined areas for entertaining. We needed green spaces for lounging and the dogs (yes, Jonathan cares more about his dogs than his own brother), a patio area for outdoor dining and another for an outdoor fire pit, plus basketball court, putting green, swimming pool, and pool house. In addition, Jonathan was insistent on installing a commercial-grade waterslide that started at the second-story loft and bottomed out in the deep end of the pool. This was the first commercial slide of its kind in a residential Vegas property. Drew was really skeptical because of the expense, but now that it's in, it's one of his favorite (and most used) features of the house. And it's awesome when we have parties. Most of our friends leave our house and then talk about the slide for weeks—instead of Drew's stellar cooking.

Not only can a great yard expand the livable space of a home, it can also increase its value. The University of Michigan did a study and discovered that home buyers value landscaped homes 11.3 percent higher than those with no or minimal landscaping. There are actually several studies that have similar findings … some cite an increase in the value of 15 percent or more. This makes sense. The first thing a buyer sees is your front yard. So it's a worthwhile investment to spend a few bucks on low-maintenance, high-quality landscaping. Just be careful not to go overboard as it's easy to blow a budget outside of your house. Greenery also lowers energy costs, as properly selected and placed trees and shrubs can substantially reduce cooling costs by shading windows from direct sunlight. Again, be careful not to go overboard …

BE SENSIBLE ABOUT LANDSCAPING. The increases in value we point out are due to savvy choices in low-maintenance plants, permanent structures (likes decks and patios), and renovations that are in keeping with the surrounding homes and overall property values. Landscaping is another place where people can really overspend and never get their money back. Keep it simple, beautiful, low maintenance, and functional, and you'll have no regrets.

First Impressions

Whether you plan to stay put for a while or know you'll move in a few years, a front yard facelift should be the first outdoor landscaping project on your list. While you'll probably spend most of your landscaping budget on your backyard, the front yard is your home's calling card and for that reason shouldn't be neglected. It's also the first impression others have of your entire home, and a bad first impression is very difficult to correct. Why not made a good one instead? Nobody wants to be the neighbor with the eyesore house! Here are some of our favorite ways to add curb appeal to your property:

1. GIVE THE FACADE A FACELIFT. A fresh coat of paint or new siding takes your home from drab to dramatic, from shopworn to show stopper. Note and repair or replace any cracked or rotted material before bringing on a house painter to finish the job. Also be aware that products like vinyl siding will actually decrease the value of a home in some communities, so be careful what materials you choose for replacement jobs, and don't sacrifice the value of the completed project just to save a few dollars up front.

2. TRIM IT. Give the front of your house a critical assessment. Would new thicker molding and trim, shutters, or more ample door casings add more gravitas to your home? Architectural details like these add visual punch to a house and give it a more substantial and stylish feel. When a homeowner replaces windows (a strong selling feature), we always want to highlight them by installing more substantial window casings, preferably something that will contrast the main exterior color. You should always emphasize any upgrades you've done in and around the house in the listing and on small placards throughout. This reinforces why a buyer should choose your place.

3. GUT IT. Oftentimes, fixer uppers have old and ineffective gutter systems that suffer from rust, peeling paint, dents, and scratches. In other words, they're ugly *and* ineffective. Replace old gutters with new snap-fit seamless gutter systems that have leaf guards and require no painting. It also means you don't have to teeter on a ladder while cleaning them out in spring and risk taking a fall. A copper system is more expensive, but for some homes, it's a style that can't be beat.

4. STEP UP. If you have blah concrete steps, topping them off with a stone veneer or tile works wonders—this is most likely a job for the pros, but it should be fairly straightforward and affordable. If wood decking leads to your front door, a power wash, new stain or porch paint, and a seal coat are a refreshing and easy facelift.

5. REDO THE DRIVEWAY. Cracked, stained driveways sprouting weeds should be repaired or replaced. There could be potential problems with uneven paving at the threshold of the garage door. It's important that grading always leads away from the house to allow for proper drainage. Asphalt is the least expensive option and is fine for many situations—but you can elevate your driveway with stamped and stained concrete, or brick or stone pavers (the most expensive). To save money but to give the appearance of a high-end driveway, use pavers as borders with more traditional concrete or asphalt. Gravel driveways can be very pretty too but require more regular maintenance and are best suited for mild climates.

6. GUSSY UP THE GARAGE DOOR. If your garage door faces the street, it's definitely part of your home's curb appeal. But even if your garage door doesn't face the street, don't neglect its care and appearance. Update plain doors with a style that includes windows and attractive hardware. Carriage-style doors look great on traditional homes; modern horizontal wood doors suit more contemporary styles. Barn-style doors look great on ranches and even on some more modern homes. Garage doors come in so many styles, there will be one in your price range to suit the look of your house. There is also a variety of lift motors available that operate silently and effectively. We prefer the side mount motors, as they are extremely quiet and do not require the bulky track and motor on your ceiling.

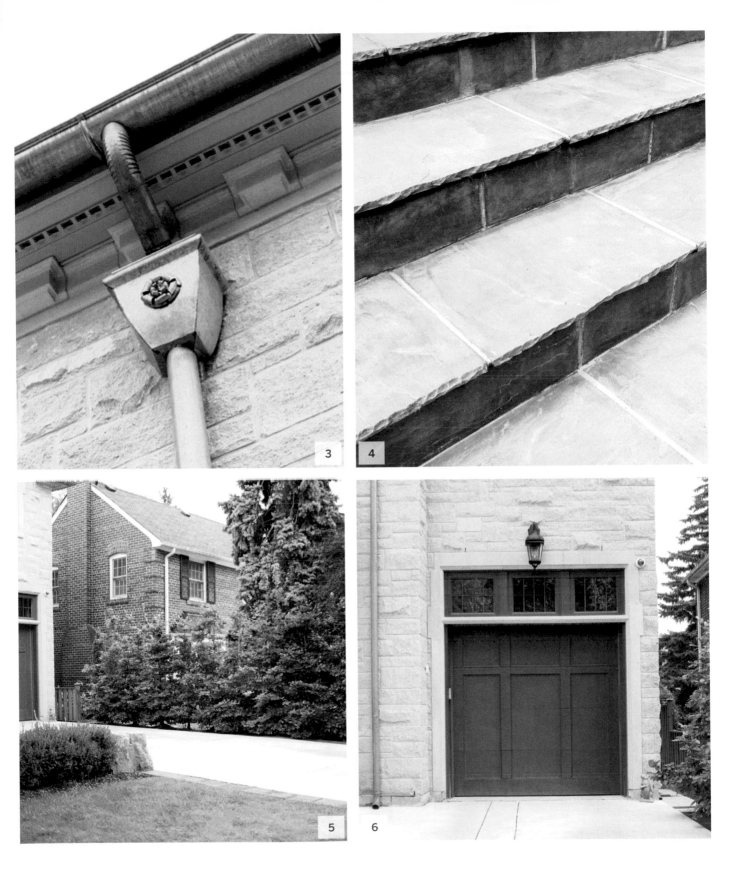

Blending the use of both hardscaping and softscaping in a balanced way creates texture, interest, and direction in a garden. Evergreens, perennials, stone, pebbles, iron, and concrete blend beautifully in these backyards.

7

8

7. PUNCH UP THE PORCH. A well-defined outdoor space in the front of a house can be really inviting. Don't pass up the potential of a porch, even a small one. Give the space purpose with stylish chairs and a side table. You could also frame the porch by adding a substantial railing in a color that contrasts with the house color and matches the trim. There isn't much we love more after a long day's work than relaxing on a beautiful porch.

8. WAKE UP YOUR WALKWAYS. Defined paths show visitors where to go and prevent people from wearing a path in your grass. Slightly curved or gently contoured paths are prettier than straight and narrow walkways. Use concrete bordered with brick or stone, or pavers. Anyone in heels can tell you how frustrating it is to walk on broken or sparse paving stones. Be sure you have laid a solid base, using sand, prior to placing your pavers, and avoid creating trip hazards.

9. JAZZ UP THE "JEWELRY." Homeowners often overlook a home's accessories—they just stop seeing them, but that doesn't mean they look good. Take a second look at your house street number; entry door lockset, knobs, or handles; wall-mounted mailbox; overhead or sconce light fixtures; shutters; and any other elements attached to the house, even something as simple as the doorbell. If they are out of date, corroded, rusty, or falling apart, replace them with fresh versions. Don't do too much mixing and matching—make sure everything you choose is cohesive in terms of style and finish. For instance, don't mix matte chrome and shiny brass. Make sure whatever you select matches the style of your home—rustic black wrought iron for a ranch style, brushed chrome for a contemporary, and oiled-bronze or un-lacquered brass for a traditional-style home.

10. LIGHT THE LANDSCAPE. Lighting makes a style statement, highlights hard or softscape and other front yard features, and provides safety and security for your home. A lit walkway, spotlights on specimen plantings, and more than one porch or front door fixture shows off your home's features and welcomes evening visitors. If you can't wire your yard, high-quality solar fixtures are a good alternative—the technology has improved over the years although they will never be quite as bright as electric lights. Battery powered LED lights last longer these days as many manufactures have incorporated automated shutoffs to save battery life.

11. FRESHEN THE FRONT DOOR. Give your entryway a color boost by replacing your ho-hum door with a beautiful one that's either stained with a rich tone or painted a bright color. One *Property Brothers* couple found the original door to their 1920s house in the garage—we were able to restore it and paint it a bright red, which really popped. An orange door against a gray or taupe facade says "welcome." A bright blue or navy door grounds a house and looks crisp with white or yellow paint. Gray and black doors are stately and traditional, but depending on the style of house they can also look sleek and modern. Green and stained wood doors are both historic-looking and rich. Yellow is cheerful and perfect for a cottage or a rustic farmhouse. The door you choose should suit the style of your house. For instance a mid-century modern paneled pine door would look better on a 1960s ranch than would a Victorian-style door with an oval leaded glass window. Screen doors and storm doors are outdated, so we recommend removing them entirely. If you can't survive without some kind of bug defense and you need to leave your door open, there are horizontal screens that tuck away neatly on the side of your door jamb.

Opt for all-season greenery, shrubs, and plants that will stay vibrant throughout the year. A focused planting approach is key. You don't need to clutter the front yard with plants to make it feel full. A garden bed lining the driveway would create a more welcoming and lush approach to the home, and a row of shrubs along the front porch would provide some privacy from the street.

12

12. MAKE YOUR BEDS. Straighten up garden beds and borders through mindful pruning and weeding, replacing struggling or dead plants, and popping in colorful annual flowers in season. Make sure any stone, brick, or block border walls are neat. Replace broken masonry work and clean dingy bricks.

---

13. PLAY WITH PLANTS. Pots and planters make a powerful statement especially when strategically placed on steps or symmetrically on either side of the door or entry to your home. If your front door is placed symmetrically, a symmetrical arrangement of pots filled with free flowing flowers, grasses, and greenery looks best—and the informal plantings will create interest within a more formal setting. For front doors set asymmetrically, an asymmetrical arrangement suits the already-dynamic setting. Having two to three planters of varied sizes and finishes can really help define a space.

14. MAKE OVER THE MAILBOX. Is your curbside mailbox sagging or rusty? Has its flag flown the coop? Maybe it's time to update it with a bigger, better, more stylish version. Choose one that complements the other hardware on your house. Paint or stain the post to match or coordinate with your home's color or front door. Next, surround it with a circle of pretty flowers or grasses—or even a climbing plant like clematis that you can easily control. If you want to ensure your mailman doesn't beat up the box, maybe leave him a little treat from time to time, in appreciation of great service.

15. THINK INSIDE THE BOX. If your home's lower floor windows lend themselves to planter boxes, consider adding them with decorative brackets. Again, make sure the boxes and brackets match the other details of your home. When planting boxes, make sure you have height (spiky grasses), fullness (impatiens or geraniums), and length (trailing ivy) for a mix of texture, dimension, and color.

16. FENCE ME IN. Jonathan is the fencing master, and he says a gate or fence around the front defines the space, gives a sense of security, and adds decoration that's also practical. There's nothing like a classic white picket fence for a traditional single story, Tudor style, cottage, or colonial-style home, but other styles of fence, from split rail for a ranch to ironwork for Victorian or modern abodes (depending on the style of iron work), offer lots of choices. Just don't erect a fence that'll make your home feel like a prison yard. Aesthetics are so important for your home—and for all of your neighbors, as it's their street too! And be sure to build a fence that will last. Most big home improvement store prefab panels start to sag and fall apart within a year. Do your homework.

17. SAY YES TO YARD ART. Weather-resistant artwork that complements your home's style brings a touch of classic elegance to its look. Fountains, birdbaths, birdhouses on tall posts, and metal, stone, or wood sculptures bring year-round interest to your front yard. In winter when plants are asleep, yard art brings structure and form to a barren yard. Just remember—don't go overboard. Carefully select and then edit your choices to be harmonious and sophisticated. You don't want your front yard to look like a junkyard. So keep those extremely "personal taste" sculptures out of drive-by sight.

CLIMATE CONTROL

Save money and time by choosing indigenous or native plants for your garden. They require less care to thrive. In our new house in Las Vegas, we chose low-maintenance native trees and shrubs that require minimal water and don't shed: The less yard work, the better. We also used artificial grass in the backyard to conserve water while still achieving that carpet of green everyone loves.

Indoor-Outdoor Living

Anything you can do to bring indoor features outside will be considered a valuable bonus to the buyer. Expanding interior spaces to the outside essentially adds extra square footage to your home's footprint and adds desirable function for entertaining and living. Here are six key concepts that will make your backyard a truly connected part of your house:

1. VIEW: If you can't see the backyard, you're probably not going to go out there very often … so make sure windows and doors in the back of your house are positioned to capture the great outdoors, so you can enjoy your yard even when you're not in it. One of the things we love about our home is the glass "wall" (accordion glass doors, really) that allows us to admire the view of the garden from the living room even when it's too hot to lounge outside.

2. FLOW: Sliders and double doors provide true indoor-outdoor living.

3. SUSTENANCE: Outdoor kitchens can be as simple or as elaborate as you like. If you're a grill champion, by all means, indulge your passion. No one ever passed up a property because the outdoor cooking station was too nice. Compact DIY outdoor kitchens now come complete with a grill, cook top, storage, and even an outdoor fridge to keep drinks icy cold. Or you can just add more presence to your grill by building an island next to it, perhaps topped with stone leftover from another outdoor project, like the patio floor, that can double as an outdoor bar and buffet.

4. FIRE: Incorporating the warmth and ambiance of real flames can be as easy as a DIY fire pit surrounded by a gravel base and simple seating, to a fancier outdoor fireplace complete with a mantel and even a pizza or bread oven. There are even great portable propane fire pits that you can place on your patio when entertaining. Whatever look or style you choose, make sure you'll get a lot of use out of it. Fire features won't always give you your money back, but they can be a great place for friends and family to gather. Fire has been encouraging socializing since we lived in caves, and you can't put a price on that.

5. WATER: Unless you live in a very warm climate, a swimming pool is probably not a plus like it is in Las Vegas (California and Florida too), but fountains and other water features, even a hot tub (which can be used year-round even in the Northeast), add soothing sounds and a visual layer to a backyard. Whether it's a birdbath or an ornamental pond with aquatic plants, this can become a focal point for your backyard living spaces and garden, or simply become a feature that helps create that Zen vibe. One important note to remember is to ensure your backyard feature doesn't consume your whole yard. It's supposed to add interest, not become the entire focal point of the backyard. The majority of buyers prefer some green space and patio area to a larger, cramping feature.

6. LIGHTING: Just as the front of your house needs lighting to brighten up its curb appeal, the backyard also needs a lighting plan. Walk through your yard and pinpoint any dark areas. You and your guests should never be stuck in a dark zone when enjoying your outdoor space. Patios and decks should be lit with either carefully placed floodlights or fixtures attached to the nearest structure, and path lights to brighten pathways and play up planting beds and specimen trees and shrubs. Don't forget about candles. Candle lanterns and candelabras work well outside, but it's also worth having the space wired for outdoor-rated lighting. You can buy LED candles that look like the real thing, but there's no worry of them ever blowing out. Solar lights, LED lights, and even outdoor lamps and chandeliers add ambiance on and over tabletops. Consider having your entire yard automated so you can control the lighting from your phone or laptop. We have split our yard into zones and moods. We can isolate the lights around the outdoor dining area or set the mood with colored low lighting surrounding the hot tub. Having this organization can make you the king of outdoor entertainers. All of these work together to create a festive mood for al fresco entertaining. Just be careful that none of your lighting shines into your neighbor's house, or you may find yourself doing damage control.

BROTHER VS. BROTHER:

Outdoor Living Rooms

JONATHAN: I'm a backyard kind of guy. So for maximum convenience, I always make sure seating areas are close to a back door so they are easy to get to. Consider the context—where possible, set your outdoor living space away from neighbors and oriented toward attractive landscaping or views. And take design cues from your house—for example, echoing its paint colors or materials to make the outdoor space feel like an extension of your home.

DREW: I like backyards too, especially a place where I can goof off and make fun of Jonathan's swimsuit fashion. But I also love to have the feeling that I'm in a "room" even when I venture outside. To achieve that, you need to bring materials and pieces that you would expect to find inside the home out into a clearly defined space. On your outdoor room's "floor" you could use a colorful exterior area rug, or even all-weather teak wood tiles that snap together. Often the house will serve as a wall or two for the outdoor room, which can be further defined with elements such as latticework, low stone or brick walls, or an arbor structure. Latticework also provides shade and privacy. We even have a wall mounted TV on one of our home's exterior walls. Furniture should be "all weather" but soft and comfortable. Be sure to have pillows too, as they finish off that internal touch. Last, give some or all of any outdoor space a roof (from wood shingles to a retractable awning) to make it more useful in rainy or damp weather.

JONATHAN: We have covered and protected outdoor spots in our Las Vegas backyard, not that it rains much in the desert. But Drew likes to protect his delicate skin ... and I like to chill in the shade. But if you don't live in the desert, you can extend your outdoor time with one of our essential outdoor elements; fire. The glow of a fire makes an outdoor room feel cozy—and extends the time you can use the space well into the fall in many climates. If you don't have room for a fireplace or pit, or your community rules have prohibitions against open flames, freestanding gas heaters—the kind you see on restaurant terraces—are now available for home use.

DREW: Furnish the space for durability and low maintenance, but treat it like a real room in terms of how you arrange seating and tables. Stylish outdoor furniture is available in every style and material and looks like it could be right at home in the family room or kitchen. Outdoor fabrics and rugs come in an ever-growing range, and look (and feel) better than ever. Substantial furniture pieces and distinctive pillows and accessories make outdoor rooms feel homey and appealing. Pick a bold accent color, perhaps drawn from flowers in your garden, for these accents.

JONATHAN: Enhance the neighboring area with additional landscaping, such as ornamental trees or bushes that can serve as a focal point or privacy screen—or a destination if visitors want to take a stroll after a meal. Vines embellish an arbor or turn latticework into green walls. Just be cautious as vines can damage a home's exterior if they run wild, so keep them contained. Adding plants to the outdoor room itself, in containers that complement your outdoor décor, provides pops of color and connects it visually to the garden. Or try filling containers with food—tomatoes, peppers, all kinds of berries, herbs, lettuces ... even potatoes grow great in containers—and you'll also have a handy source of food all summer long.

DREW: Outdoor speakers add to the fun and versatility of your outdoor room. There's no excuse not to have a party, but respect your neighbors and keep the volume at a reasonable level.

YOU *CAN* HAVE
Your Dream Home

We'll always remember one renovation in particular. We worked with a single dad who had five kids. He was struggling to pay the bills and keep a roof over his children's heads—a roof on a house that was way too small for the family. He wanted to find a way to put money aside for his kids' college funds but he just didn't know where or how to begin. He actually thought saving for college was unrealistic.

This fellow tried selling his too-small home with the hope that the proceeds from a sale could help pay down his debts, as well as help move his family into a better situation. Unfortunately, the house needed so many repairs that no one wanted to take a chance. We worked with him to help his plans come to fruition. First, we fixed all the minor concerns in his house, which included some plumbing problems and repairs to walls and floors. We also updated the place to give it some sought-after features, such as a modern kitchen and extra storage. We even helped him organize a plan to reduce his debt load.

The house sold in one day for more than the asking price. The sale gave the home-owner enough money to fund a college account, pay off his debts, and afford a down payment on a bigger home just outside his current neighborhood. The process didn't just transform his home; it transformed his life. This was a very emotional sale for him, as he never thought in a million years that he could pull himself out of his drowning debt.

This is the change that can happen when you undertake a savvy home improvement project—and we hope you've been inspired by what we've laid out in this book. You'd be surprised what you can accomplish with a positive attitude. One of our favorite sayings is, "Doubt kills more dreams than failure ever will." This great quote taught us to never fear trying something different. We know you can do it. We've helped so many people, so many families, realize the potential that their home has. We feel blessed to have the ability to affect people all around the world in a positive way and give them the opportunity to live in a way they never thought possible. Everyone deserves to live in his or her dream home, no matter how that is defined. Being a part of helping homeowners transform their lives is something we will always enjoy.

We hope *Dream Home* has inspired you to take a chance and reach for the kind of house and life you want and deserve. We might bicker and argue and poke fun at each other but at the end of the day, we're family. Our parents taught us that a house is truly a home when it's filled with family, friends, and love. That's the idea that underlies all of our renovations and designs. Take that feeling with you into your own projects. Good luck!

ACKNOWLEDGMENTS

The process of creating this book has been a journey that goes back long before we ever put pen to paper. Prior to filming the first episode of *Property Brothers*, and even earlier than buying our first investment property at age 18. It has been an undertaking that in many ways mirrors how we produce our shows. We're often asked how it's possible that we pull off these incredible transformations all by ourselves. The simple fact is, we don't. With every series we shoot, there's an orchestra of incredible individuals who work tirelessly to support bringing our vision to life. This book—and the development of every thought on its pages—is no different. Here are some of the people who have been instrumental in helping us get to this point.

Our mom and dad, Joanne and James Scott, have supported every outlandish idea our overachieving minds could dream up. Whether it was starting our hanger business at 7 years old, or purchasing a fixer-upper that looked ready to condemn ... they kept an open mind. They nurtured our entrepreneurial spirit, but reminded us to take pause and always consider how our actions affect those around us. We were constantly reminded that the path to success involves a lot of hard work, and no shortcut is worth compromising our integrity. Yes, our parents "created us," however the true testament to their commitment in making us who we are today is how they've never stopped guiding and encouraging us in the 38 years following our birth.

Our big brother, our best friend, JD Scott, has always been there as the calm voice of reason in a sometimes chaotic world. Though as children he found us utterly unbearable ... as adults, we couldn't be closer. He taught us to be adventurous, spontaneous, and kind. On occasion he would lead us by mischievous bad example ... haha ... however, he most often paved the way in the right direction. He's the guy who's right by our side whether we are up or down. The first person we call during any major life moment, and the only guy we'd ever be in a pop country boy band with ... again ;)

After many, many years of growing our real estate/construction business, Scott Real Estate, and endless pitches to various networks and production companies about our operation, we're incredibly thankful for the one that returned our call. Cineflix has been an amazing partner since the beginning and really allowed us to do what we do best. They went out on a limb to try a show idea that hadn't been done before and work with two young guys sporting questionable hair. The gamble paid off and we have managed to produce two hit series with them that now reach more than 140 countries and territories.

Over the years we have developed an incredible team of people at our production company, Scott Brothers Entertainment, who are the best in their fields. No matter how high we raise the bar, these folks always exceed our expectations. We've produced countless award-winning and engaging shows, many of which we're in and others where we've developed new talent. We only work with people we like to work with—and we like these people a lot.

No series can be a success without the right network partners. In our case it took two. W Network in Canada and HGTV in the U.S. have been instrumental in growing the shows and allowing us to constantly evolve in order to lead the genre. They allow us the creative freedom to try new things, but also the guidance and expertise we need to understand what audiences are looking for. These people have been our longtime business partners, but have also become our friends. You know when you karaoke and ride mechanical bulls with them ... it's going to be a long, fulfilling relationship.

Our agency, CAA, has also been instrumental in shaping our brand and developing strategy that keeps us constantly looking beyond to see what our next big step should be. Matthew Horowitz was the first person to suggest we take this wealth of knowledge we have and shape it into a book. He introduced us to Cait Hoyt, who has been our biggest advocate and the backbone of this entire process. Even though there have been ups and there have been downs ... Matt and Cait still answer our calls ;)

For this book specifically, we were fortunate enough to work with an incredible team that really knew exactly how to focus our ideas to maximize the take away info for the reader. Whether it was the stunning photography by David Tsay; Karen Kelly who successfully concentrated all our wild ideas; our eyes and ears throughout the whole project, Lisa Canning; and especially our incredible crew at Houghton Mifflin Harcourt (Justin Schwartz, Rebecca Liss, Brad Thomas Parsons, Allison Renzulli, Marina Padakis Lowry, Tom Hyland, and Tai Blanche) who were determined to make this the best book it could possibly be. We couldn't have done it without them.

Finally, words cannot express how important this last thank you is. It's to you. Our fans have proven time and time again to be this incredibly passionate group of individuals who not only support every endeavor we embark on, but also rally behind us to make our ventures a success. We listen to you, we laugh with you, and we truly do integrate your suggestions into our shows. We have never experienced anything like the relationship we have with our fans. We are who we are because of you. Thank you for letting us into your homes. Thank you for making us a part of your lives.

Index